LOVE, LOVE AT THE END

PRAYER
FROM
THE
CATbIRd
Seat

MY GOD

FOR A SPACE OF DAYS
reFUSE MY gAMES
BE YOURSELF MERCILESSLY
BE SeRIOUS IN THE WORLD   SAY GREAT THINGS IN
STAND UNWAVERING
BESIDE THE FAULTY AND PERPLEXED
SPEAK MODESTLY   ACT AUDACIOUSLY   SING F
bE FORBEARING AND EQUAbLE
                                UNdER ObSCEN

WHERE RUMOR ALLOWS ONLY EVIL
                                            WIDEN

THE NO MAN'S WASTE OF HATREd
                              YES,

                    STRIKE GENTLY
                    THE STRINGS OF INARTICULATE
                                        HEARTS

FOR YOU   LIFE
          IS NEITHER   MIRAGE NOR ABSU
                              BUT SUPERS
                                  AVAILA
                                  OVERF

OF STRENGTH AND COMPASSION   A RUNNEL SO PURE IT CL
                    THE INTOLERABLE STABLES OF OUR FOU

SO DEEP WE ARE CARRIED ALONG   DROWNED AND

AN ENCOMPASSING LOVE WE LIVE AND MOVE IN

            METAMORPHOSED OUT OF OUR SWEET

ARE YOU

EAST OR WEST   POOR OR IN POSSESION

SQUATTER IN WATTS SOMNOLENT SUBURBAN ROTTING IN JAILS YES
                                                            ALLOWING

VICIOUS DEPRADATIONS   AGAINST
                      BONES AND FLESH OF BROTHERS?

BE ANSWER BE QUESTION !
       WHEN OR WHERE
     ARE YOU ABSENT O
TERMAGANT OF HISTORY TIGER OVERARCHING
               WITH YOUR ELECTRIC BODY OUR SKIES

UNFENDED CHILDHOOD INTELLECTUAL GRANDEUR SCOPE BEYOND OUR COMPASS!

       COME EASTER

FLOWERS BIRDS FLYING TREES AND MEN
INFLAME WITH YOUR MOUTH TO MOUTH
           RESPIRATION   THE MORTKIAN SMILE OF DEATH

      COME PEACE AND SWORD
   bREAK THE LOCKED FISTS OF DOMINATIONS
                   UPON OUR THROATS
      COME SURGEON DRAW INTO ONE
  CUNNING ANTHROPOS THE BONES BONES DRY BONES
  SLACK JAWS SCATTERED KNEES
             OF THE AMNESIAC DEAD

    COME DESERT SUN

    SUCK INTO NOTHING
            OUR BRACKISH SERPENTINE
                 JOYS

    COME STIGMATIC

WRITE ON OUR FOREHEADS
OUR BLUE EYEBALLS
  WORDS YOU SCRAWLED
      ON DEATH'S
      HIDEOUS LIMBS

  WHERE NONE BUT YOU ESCAPED
        HIS OVERKILL ARROGANT
           REACH

GLORY GLORY GLORY

NT

AND VICTIMIZED
IN THE TEETH OF THE LAW

S

EE GOOD

ION   REDUCE TO ZERO

Daniel Berrigan, S.J.

LOVE,
LOVE
AT THE END

*Parables, Prayers and
Meditations*

THE MACMILLAN COMPANY, *NEW YORK, NEW YORK*

COLLIER-MACMILLAN LIMITED, *LONDON*

The author wishes to thank the following for permission to reproduce copyrighted material: *The Critic* for "Prayer for the Big Morning," "Prayer for the Morning Headlines," "Prayer from a Back Pew," "Prayer from the Catbird Seat," "Prayer from a Picket Line," "Prayer of the Third Man," "Prayer on the Six P.M. Subway," "Suburban Prayer," February–March 1966, Vol. XXIV, No. 4; *The Critic* for "Alas," "Boy and the Tiger," "Death and the Bishop," "The First Days of the Science of Prenatal Communication," "Irene," "The Shoes That Failed," "The Statue," April–May 1967, Vol. XXV, No. 5; *The National Catholic Reporter* for "Meditation on a Photograph," December 21, 1966.

Library of Congress Catalog Card Number: 68-12280

First Macmillan Paperbacks Edition 1971
Second Printing 1971

The Macmillan Company
866 Third Avenue, New York, N.Y. 10022
Collier-Macmillan Canada Ltd., Toronto, Ontario
Printed in the United States of America

Jack AND *Mary Lewis*

LOVE TO THE END

CONTENTS

II PRAYERS

III MEDITATIONS

I PARABLES

NO CUTTING LOOSE

A MAN ONCE found himself bound by his feet to a shadow who talked and talked back.

After long probing, an analyst declared that his skill was useless. There was no cutting loose.

The man went on living, nonetheless, a kind of drama, a kind of defeat. With every sunny day, he was exposed under the merciless noonday, midstage. He had never cast himself as a protagonist, but his shadow forced the issue, giving his colorless and self-condemned existence a kind of neutral radiance. Its glory was neither great nor evil nor seductive, but it isolated him and rendered him, by the dark presence of an opposite number, incandescent, solitary, a sour spontaneous bloom in a desert. In such a landscape, he was man, he was the only man, the only possible man.

It was very nearly unbearable. He wore his body like an aching organ whose nerve ends had a separate intelligence, fused to his own as questioned to questioner. Why do I suffer? Why cannot I be at peace? Or like a child whose term is long past, who will not slumber and cannot be born—Why am I here? Where are you bearing me?

He would seek out sunless corners and long for cloudy

days. Then his shadow would curl up like a sleeping animal at his breast, its breathing would melt into his own. But it had a vivid dream life, and tossed in its sleep, and told what it saw. And sometimes the things it saw in darkness were more terrifying than the things it questioned in the sun. I see, I see, it would begin, and the man would shake in a spasm of anquish, knowing that he must see it too. I see the landscape of hell. I have landed on the moon, I am without a way for return. I see a flower dying; give me water.

Sometimes, rarely, he knew a period of relief. It came about in the strangest way. It seemed that hands, his own hands, the hands of his shadow, removed the foul burden of his clothing, lifted his skull like a steel casque and put it on, dismembered his bones and stepped into them. He was left insubstantial and airy and weightless, free alike of impure joy and false hope, the dark lees of his blood drained away, his spirit dry and resonant as a bleached shell. Hell and earth and heaven—what were these to him? He became at such times like the sunlight. He created his own shadow. The cock of his eye made long men and short, fat men and thin. He exalted and rode high, he circled heaven like an imperial bird, he conferred crowns and dispensed life. Men and their shadows lived in the mighty circumference of his love. Come, he whispered, be silent, be free, be gods.

Was he playing God? Was he dangerous? Let us say no; because he must also return to his skin, and play man again, and be helpless, and wrestle with despair.

Clothing, bones, skull, shadow, they hung on a nail on the wall, awaiting morning. The dawn came; he awoke and sighed and arose to life once more.

IRENE

THERE WAS ONCE a dove named Irene, who had learned in a Montessori school to say the word "peace." A spectacular success! When Irene would sing out the word, it was evident that she was totally committed. Her beak would redden, her plumage would stand up like cat's fur in a wind.

Then Irene took to smoking L & M's. This was a new phase in her peace work. She shortly was able, in a reasonably quiet room, to spell "peace" in smoke, in midair.

Various peace groups heard of the feat. Overtures were made. It was revealed that for a very modest stipend, or no stipend at all, Irene would spell 'peace' in smoke at peace gatherings. And not long after, more deeply committed than ever, she came on a brilliant idea. She would train a whole team of sky girls to spell 'peace' in smoke in the open air.

Once the idea was explored, it became clear that its horizons were unlimited. At one protest march, Irene and her girls, now grown to a dazzling team of fifty, with fifty stand-ins, spelled 'peace' in letters one hundred feet high above Manhattan. The act all but eclipsed the parade itself.

Soon after, however, tragedy struck. Irene and her girls suddenly disappeared. A few stragglers from her second team were still to be seen in Manhattan, scrounging in Central Park and City Hall Square. Rumors went thick and fast; Irene had been shot down, Irene had been subverted. Among Manhattan pigeons, a few, sharper of eye and leaner of hip than the others, took notes with transistor recorders. They pieced the rumors together and came on the truth. Irene and her girls could be found at a heavily guarded armory on the west side. She was preparing a new show, under security wraps as tight as any devised by Billy Rose. For a price, someone knew a way in, high up under the steel beams of the roof.

The price was paid. Two agents, posing as tourists, but fitted from foot to wing with electronic equipment, got through with their guide.

Inside, the air was heavy with a pall of smoke, noisy as a midtown athletic club. Irene's voice rang out, high above all the rest; she was piercing and quick as a hawk, diving and swooping among her team. A final practice was about to start; the doves lined up. Irene shrieked a signal. From the floor, almost vertically, fifty white doves went up. They had been fitted with whistle-devices in their tails, with beaks and spurs of steel. They screamed like sky bolts, broke formation with blinding speed, then loosed a jet of smoke as white as their plumage. The message, "Bomb the hell out of Hanoi."

MY SON JOHN

THERE WAS ONCE a child who used to play only in the front yard, where everyone was like himself. One day, however, after a passage at arms with a younger brother, he was sent for punishment into the back yard.

Back yard? He hadn't known there was one. A sea change, a revelation! Tanners, shoemakers, alleys, gutters, children, wash women, markets, flower carts, beggars. There was not much time for tears. The child sat on the back stoop half frightened, totally fascinated.

After a while he was in the thick of it, playing with the others; after a few hours he too was dirty and joyful. It was as though a sprite, benign and mischievous, had led him blindfolded into a place of delights, and then whisked the darkness away.

His exile ended, as such things will. He was called back indoors, and on into the front yard. He went in with a new look on his face. He knew something for the first time. It had come to him with the delicacy and unpredictability of lightning, with the logic of nature, of water and sun, of the opening of a door. He knew now, that a front yard existed because a back yard existed. He knew alternatives; in the name of punishment, a dangerous gift was in his hands. Front will have back, rich will have poor, master will have slave, pride will have fall, blood will have blood.

He could also do sums in a new way. I mean, he would cry aloud in later years, I know why our ladder has fifty rungs. I know how we got up and stay up. I know whose filth and sweat make us smell like roses. I mean bodies, cordwood, something to walk on, human lives, good stupid rungs of wood locked in place, steady in the middle, tight in the socket, dumb, petrified. Count them, climb them, walk on them!

The boy went back indoors and got washed and admonished and kissed and came out the front door. Does he now smell like roses, look like his mother, talk like his father? Is he fervent for one kind of justice, which is to say, for his kind of injustice? Is he clean as a cravat, a good business head, ready for law or medicine or army—or chancery?

What had he lost; what had he gained? Was he tamed, housebroken, the rich kid unsulled by the barnyard, a good metallurgic triumph, papa's pride, mama's sacramental, the lion who lies down on command, the ambulatory hearthside rug?

No. The story has a happy ending. State didn't win. Neither did church. Nor papa nor mama nor dominations nor powers, nor fat ease nor lean revenge, nor height nor breadth nor depth. Our story has a happy ending. Which is to say:

The boy stood above the dirty water that had collected in a broken street. And he did a very simple thing. He took off his clothes. All the little boys and girls had done the same thing. They stood there together in the silence of an epiphany. The boy took off his clothes, and he saw himself. And he saw the world.

I see, he said, a boy looking back at me, a boy who is like myself; two hands, two arms, two eyes, a hairy head, a thingummy between two legs. I can scoop up dirty water and throw it. I can wade in. I can wade deeper. I can get in over my head. I can pee gently. Why, the whole world is like myself, looking back, smiling, frowning, mugging, pushing, joining hands, dancing. And getting hungry, and staying hungry. And sweating (he went on—because he stood there for years—the thing really had no end) and suffering, sinning, rejoicing, marrying, child bearing. And dying. And so on and so on.

The boy came back to the front lawn, to the tranquil house, to the poodles and terriers and doormen. But he was never again the same. How could he be? The question in his eyes was the measure of his awakening. It was himself; he was a question to himself. To ask the question at all was dangerous, as dangerous as it was to be alive. To listen to answers, to be grateful for help, to seek light in his perplexity—all this he did, and more. But the more was all the difference. For every answer fed the question. The fire could never be put out, never again.

How to be man, how to be himself, how to be messenger, how not to forget the message, how to bring the good news or the bad news from the back yard into the front yard? Ah, he had broken through.

Men, beware a man.

CR✗D

DEATH AND THE BISHOP

O NCE, A BISHOP was accosted in public by Death.
My lord, would you have a minute to spare?

The Bishop, who was a hearty man in public, thought
he would.

Would you by any chance have a smoke on you?
The Bishop who was a chain smoker, but not in public,
handed one over.

And Bishop (Death's skinny hand was now on my
lord's coat), could you spare the price of a cup of
coffee?

The Bishop thought he could, but less heartily. He
strove to end the interview, and to pass on. His day was
a busy one.

Death clung to him. My lord, he whined, a poor man
needs a coat. The winds are chill, even to an unbeliever.

This was pushing a bit hard. But they were in public,
and a crowd was gathering. The Bishop, who was not
beyond a gesture, had heard of St. Martin of Tours,
though he had no ambitions in that direction. He took
off his coat. Death put it on. The Bishop's hat as well.
And his shoes. And his socks. And his ring. And Death
went on his way, humming the "Alleluia" from Handel.

In the days that followed, Death had cause to marvel

at his improved situation. People kissed his ring with fervor, his public relations warmed. Indeed a religious revival began to make itself felt.

And a small matter, heretofore thought unpleasant, took a visibly turn for the better. Instead of violence and long wasting and absurd eventuality, Death adopted the paternal liturgy of a bishop. Men came to him willingly. And a slight blow on the cheek, a gesture of confirmation, sufficed. Things ended satisfactorily for many. There was talk of a larger See, a more ample scope for this promising and adaptive person.

THE SAD ONE

THERE WAS A mournful typewriter, and this was its complaint. If only someone loved me! Alas. Alas. I am uncovered at nine, I am covered at five, like a captive bird. No poetry, no music, no freedom songs, no declarations of independence. I cannot see who passes in the street or who dies in the house or who weeps beyond the walls. I have never conferred a name on a newborn child, I have never had a leaf fall on me, or sat under a tree in bloom. No one takes me to the park. But every day a bored girl limbers me up, and begins to play out her sour soul on my keys. I am dying of it, and so is she.

Some day I am going to write her a love letter:

My dear, my dear, don't give up. Someone loves you. Not a harassed clerk or a harassing boss. Not a necktie or a filing cabinet or a discreet smirk. Not a paycheck, or an expense account. But someone, someone.

Will you seek him? Listen. Follow the clues. Go, when you read this, to the old apple tree at the corner of Unpleasant and Fruitless. Stand there, listen to the leaves. Then hold out both hands. Something beautiful will fall or fly to them. A clue. Open it. Sing its words. Follow, follow, follow.

THE BOY AND THE TIGER

A YOUNG GOD once created for his pleasure, on the fourth day of the week, a tiger cub. On the fifth and sixth day, the boy was more than usually occupied. He returned home on Sunday to share his rest with his new pet.

The day was a delight. The two played and walked in the temperate weather of the garden. The cub was everything the god had hoped for—wisdom, insouciance, innocent and unawakened violence. When in the course of their play the tiger scratched the god's arm, both stopped and smiled and the tiger licked the blood away.

However, the second week went less well. The cub grew restive. He took to moping in corners, began to scratch himself, and turned away from vegetables. And one morning when the boy awoke, he found the tiger had wet the floor thoroughly, set up a sign nearby reading, "Freedom now," and disappeared. He was gone for three days. He finally lurched in again, with a wicked gleam in his eye and liquor on his breath. He slept all that day and his dreams must have been pleasant ones, for he snickered and belched in his sleep.

The god went to his father, in tears. But the father was in no mood to dispense sympathy. "You wanted a tiger, you made a tiger, now live with him. Or if you can't, turn him into a rug or a humming bird. I have my own troubles. The gardeners are on strike, and a snake from somewhere is organizing a union."

To cage the beast was to violate their agreement. The tiger knew it and took advantage of it. One night he got into the chicken coops and disposed of five prize Rhode Island reds. Then he sat in the garden for two hours, roaring at the moon. The other animals were terrified. Many of them fled for good. The others began muttering about violence in the street and arming themselves.

The boy did his best. He took to reading the tiger long passages from the Sermon on the Mount. He pointed with modesty to his own record of nonviolence, and read passages from a handbook he was composing. He recited from memory the Chinese and Hindu poets, with special emphasis on the Zen ideal of the tiger who changed his stripes.

All this took a long time, and endless virtue. Finally the boy's patience seemed to be winning. The tiger grew more thoughtful. He wept frequently and asked for the sacrament. He was also growing older; his sleek coat faded, his teeth fell out. Then one morning, when the boy brought out the tiger's breakfast, he found no tiger at all, but a newborn lamb lying on an old tiger's skin. The boy gathered the lamb in his arms. Now at last he understood.

But he did not understand. A few days after, the lamb also disappeared.

In a remote field, sick at heart after a long search, the boy came upon his pet, reduced to fleece, tail and hooves. Nearby was a message in the old tigerish hand, written in lamb's blood.

"Dear friend," it said, "sorry. Consult Spinoza, volume three, question four: On the Persistence of Evil in the World. . . ."

I AM A STATUE in a church, dusted by a crazy warden. He prays to me, he lights candles before me. And you do not know what it means; the dead at the mercy of the living. Every day they come to ask for virtues I know nothing of. And who ever conferred on others a life he never lived, a gift he never possessed? Magic, magic, a blank check. "Please make me better, please bring my lover back, please get me off the hook, please take me off the bottle."

Death-ridden people, the cure of the world lies within the world; only life is the healer of life. Let me tell you of my pain; it is not to be what you are, it is not to suffer what you endure.

I offer one solution, to your quandary and mine. Burn the bones of the dead. Remember us by forgetting us. There is one gift, life itself; morning and evening, foul weather and good, the cry of childbirth, the last breath of the dying. Love, love life. Die, loving life.

THE TOOLS

I REMEMBER A BOY and his father and a set of tools.

But first of all, to push the question back, as the boy often did in his own mind, a question of beginnings. How had it begun? Once, his father was a young lover, a new husband. And he saw in his wife's eyes a question, a tease, an invitation. And he launched on the deep, a good voyage, all sheets to the wind. The moon was honey, the wind stood fair. He loved a woman, he could not imagine himself without her love. She was wind and port and sail and rudder and anchor, all in one.

Then, a question of tools, as we said. The making of a son, the making of a home. Imagine a man—skilled in love, which is an art; in making things, which is also an art. And the pride he takes in his tools—order and cleanliness and guardianship. Jealousy? Well, certainly pride, with the dangers that shadow a good thing. Pride, preference, solitude. Kids keep out! But he never put up a sign.

The boy eyed the tools, and watched his father, and awaited his chance. Can I try it, can I make something?

Well . . . We'll start with something harmless, something unbreakable. The boy might get the knack. A knife without a blade, a hammer with a rubber head, a wrench that grabs nothing. He'll learn. Stretched out on the floor or crawling around the floor, fooling with blocks and curlers and sawdust.

Then one day, it's no longer funny or cute. The boy can no longer be put off. He wants—reasonably, acutely, persistently, as a dog wants a bone, as a fish water, as a bird air—he wants to make something. He wants the feel of a tool in his hand. Outrageous—he wants the feel of the world.

The dilemma that arises is the father's. He is neither wise nor great nor infallible. I deny it, because I wish you to know him adequately. I wish you to know where he begins and where he leaves off, the edges, the substance of a beautiful life. I am denying, you see, that this man is God. Though I am affirming with equal insistence that he is like God.

But my main point is one of tools—a God who makes a world. A God who unlocks the universe and hands out the tools of creation to the men who line up. And a father who resembles this God because the man, too, has made something—a house, a son, a table. And perplexed too like God, in his partial wisdom; because his son stands before him and will not be put off. So the father must, like it or no, smile. And with many reservations at heart, say to his son: "go ahead! try it!"

The boy does. A catastrophe. The hammer swings from his unsteady wrist like a demolition ball on a cable. This way and that, wrong, crooked, split, a purple thumb in a bandage.

And what about my tools? He pounds a nail in crooked, bends it over at the head, and uses the nail as landmark for a saw blade. The blade sings in the wood, hits the nail with a howl like a dervish. The father holds it up, a ruined Excalibur. He will hear its wail raking his spine for days. What will that boy ever amount to?

He can't even take care of my tools. He leaves the place a shambles. I found a wrench in the wet grass— I mean the blade of the mower found it. I'm going to lock things up again. The experiment's gone wrong. He'll never make anything!

A moment of truth. Does the father see his blood turning dark, his confidence gone sour, a boy whose hand is reaching too far, a threat? The boy who begins to stake his claim—to what? To equal height, to a place in the sun, to cast a long shadow—to be wrong?

I had a dream, the father said to himself. The boy was in the back yard, with his jackknife in hand, playing that game he calls Territory. He cast the knife and carved a big slice out of the wet earth. And when I looked down— I stood within. There I was on his land, in his house, at his table, in his bed. I was old and dry as a stick. I sat on a bedpan and smelled the paper roses. He fed me, he wiped my behind, he buried me. I lie in his land claim, shoved into his ground. *Requiescat*, he said like a spoiled priest, good riddance. God is dead; I drove the nail into the lid with his own hammer.

It is the father's dream I am telling. I must state it strongly. Because I defend the son, whose life is my only competence, whom alone I know. And I say to the father as his son does. My father, I do not understand you. Allow me to love you. Pay the price. Love me.

THE CATECHUMENS

THE CODE WAS "butter."

We have a shortage of bombs, a general fumed. I'll cable Washington.

How is it—stop, great society—stop, highest standard of living, etc.—stop, cannot keep us supplied with butter—stop. How butter up these villages, crops, cattle, children, suspected v.c.—stop. without butter?—stop. Please inform —stop.

So Washington got with it. A call went out to the world capitals, discreet pressures were exerted, hints were dropped, embassy wires hummed. Stores of bombs, long forgotten, were uncovered once more. Jordan, it was disclosed, had bombs buried along the Negeb under six feet of sand, in potholes six feet apart. Nasser had a store piled in an abandoned mosque. They were stamped, strangely enough, "Israel"; whether in reference to fabricant or destinant no one would say. West Germany had bombs lying on their noses in a remote Bavarian spa, in four feet of water. They were hauled out for testing, and though rusty, were found to be in good working order. They had, it developed, been sold to the Germans for $2.80 apiece. They could be bought back for $22.00

apiece. This, as Bonn explained, would ease the mark shortage and spread the butter further.

So bombs in crates stamped "butter" began to arrive at . . . (censored).

Meantime, back in the developing nation, the people under the bombs grew more and more puzzled. Each day the planes went over; day after day. And no bombs fell. Villagers poked their heads out of their huts, out of shelters they had dug in tree roots and out of the sides of cliffs. They picked up the leaflets that had fallen like manna. The pages showed smiling, crewcut airmen, their arms loaded with gifts. Underneath, the caption, "We butter while we build." In smaller print, the architect of the new world had written a personal message:

> People, bear with us. The temporary shortage of butter is traceable not to us, but to enemies of your country and ours, for whom our common enterprise means nothing. Peace, Justice, Good Fortune. We shall return.

The pigs crept about, rooting in the sunshine. Here and there in the scorched land, a few shoots of green appeared. Copters bearing movie stars and folk rock bands came in. The evenings were lit by klieg lights, the villages rang with music and song. On stage, an American queen in her fishnet shimmered and exulted, captive and captivating, the sacred fish at the altar, the heart of our effort. Around her, in packed rows, the major and minor organs of a new world body; generals, pacifiers, engineers, soldiers in fatigues.

And at the edges, like catechumens seeking access to the mystery, the villagers in rags. Once it was Visigoths,

Celts, Huns; now the rude village Buddhists. History would win. A great Christian nation, "extending her arms in a deeply felt religious faith" warmed to the electric touch of destiny. All was well with the world, our world, and God's. All manner of things would be well.

ALLELUIA!

THERE WAS ONCE a man who died, and rose again to life.

He had been a suburban man. He remembered trudging the open fields, a Saturday in the country. Had he been struck by lightning? Had a bull charged him? He recalled a streak of horror coming through broken fences, crowned with daisies, demonic and bloodshot. His groin felt as though it had been ripped into by a scythe.

He stood up. No fields, no space, no landmarks. A city street. Cold. A musty doorway. His coat and face and hands covered with a dust of snow. Dazed and drunk, two legs under him like sticks of wood.

It was a city street, night, and infernal cold. The neon went off and on down the canyon, a bleary charade of eyes.

He shook like a dog, and took a few steps. The plate glass of a bar window drew him. He looked, and looked again. What was it, what face looked back? Black face? His mouth froze in a scream, his voice stuck in his throat. The neon winked him off and on, made and destroyed him, the ugliest joke of all creation. A black face held him; it said like a bad joke, like a truthful ad; don't buy me. Danger. I'm poison. I don't beautify.

Beware. No one recommends me, no family sings for me. Beware.

His hands went to his throat. A string of cheap beads. To his chest; two breasts. A whore's careless dress, a sack of anguish. A woman? Who died there? What arose here?

And then the neon took voice, the night erupted. A band of herald angels from the sewers, from the skies, sang this birth. "Welcome, sister, to a new skin. Welcome to the other side. Why, you're now two-thirds of all of us; black. The other half of us, woman. Black woman. What piety, what merits won this rebirth?" For country acres, for country matters, for wise polity, for good acts and good investments, this reward. For that I was hungry and you knew me not, I was thirsty and you gave me no drink. Welcome. Not to punishment, not to hell. To a new chance. To a new body, to the new city.

Now, at length, I love you. Now I choose you. Welcome, outcast, reject, welcome to cold and fear and exhaustion and the dead end of corrupt hope. I anoint you and summon you, I kiss you with the kiss of my lips. Arise my love, my dove, my beautiful one.

THE SINGLE ROSE

An old woman looked out from an etching entitled "Old Woman." Her face was dark as blood in moonlight. So the artist had seen her, and so she approved what he saw, and triumphed for him, lending her dark life to his eyes and hands. She sat there, his skill and her reality. Dark, dark, her eyes lowered, her skin blackened in time's acid, her look turned inward. She wore an old shirt, open at the throat, a bandana was folded about her forehead, tied at the back. She was ugly and serene, a dense clarity enveloped her; age, attrition, silence.

From her body, children had been drawn. Now they walked on their own. Her arms had been skilled in the order and disorder of love. But she had let it all go. Her body slumped forward. Her life was a drought-stricken exodus, she sat in a rickety cart holding the reins of a winded and broken horse, going nowhere.

An icon? You could not imagine cherubs upbearing her or incense smoking around her. No apotheosis sprang from her eyes, her virtue asked nothing, would receive nothing of this world. Death was on her face, she was riding toward a landscape of clouds and gray earth. You could see her pulling on the reins, getting down, falling where she stood. You could hear the ill-fitting hinge closing, and the earth falling on the lid. She invited the kiss of dissolution, she was shadowed by her dark lover, Lord Riddance to rubbish, dust to dust.

And I could not bear with it. So I set her image in a decent chair, and went out from the house at nightfall, and bought a single rose to place before her. I would not have her altered for all the world. But I must alter the world, in small measure, for her sake. I must create around, for the sake of that perfection which time and pain and weathers had wrought of her, a measure of harmony in which she might dwell, for at least an evening.

She may look up yet, and smile crookedly, and wink. She is capable of anything.

ALAS

THERE WAS ONCE a man afflicted with hemorrhoids. And he would fain have them shrunken. One day, in a subway, providence raised his eyes to an ad. It read: "Preparation H Shrinks Hemorrhoids."

The man lost no time. He tore his eyes from the evangel of hope, he hurried to buy, and to begin treatment.

Alas, in the onset of his joy, he read the instructions wrong.

Yet the fault had its compensation. Now his head is of manageable size; his hats cost him less, as do his ideas. And if his trouble remains, he thinks about it less.

THE SHOES THAT FAILED

ONCE THERE WAS an elephant. He was unique only in this; whether he walked or stood, he leaned to the left. Not far to the left, since his center of gravity was a matter of tons, and could not be seriously tampered with. But visibly off-center, whether by fault or triumph in nature, men were not agreed.

When he was led out for peace marches he leaned to the left and was cheered for it.

But when a political party hired him for its convention, matters were different. He was booed and hissed, elements of the right cried, "Traitor," and called for his removal.

His owners were no ideologists. But they could smell a good thing, and this animal smelled sweet indeed. So they made for him a pair of interchangeable elevator shoes, colored gray to match his complexion. He would wear them on his short side, fore and aft, on conservative occasions, and on his long side, to introduce a note of danger, for movements of the left. The option was tried. He was led out, teetering like a drunken calliope, to protest a foreign landing by our troops. But in the midst of the consequent uproar, the beast fell, and that was that. It cost an enormous sum to hoist him upright. The elephant emerged shaken in his psyche, and more determined to be himself.

Shortly thereafter, however, animal symbols fell from favor altogether. Instead, the war parties paraded with phalanxes of paper cannons, which discharged war bonds into the air. The peace lovers devised cornucopias that discharged drum majorettes chanting the beatitudes.

Galled and disheartened, the animal was sold; his flesh for rendering, his tusks, hooves and tail for whatever they would bring. He metamorphosed into history, mingling with the absurd options which time pretends to clarify. In vain! He became boots for the military, ivory for leisurely hours of chess, chemical agents, aphrodisiacs, vitamins, floor wax and buttons. After the mockeries of time, his real life was under way.

THE TEMPTER

THERE WAS ONCE a man who carried a tempter on his back. The Thing was the size of a black squirrel with a nearly human face. He used his forked tail for a third hand; he spoke six languages in a voice like a drama coach.

One day the two were walking companionably in Central Park. The Thing as usual was badgering the man. "Look at yourself," he said in English, "you'll be forty-six years old on May 9th, and what have you to show for it?"

The man did what he was told. He closed his eyes and looked. He saw nothing new; a pleasant slob with an unpressed look, a life that was now pleasant, now hellish, but mostly gray. But he said nothing, being resigned to the sight.

The two turned north at the edge of the lagoon. The man suddenly had an idea. "Get behind my eyes," he said softly, "and you'll see what I have to show for it." He stretched out his arms, scooped up the pool in his hands, held the waters a moment like a libation, and then tossed them over his left shoulder. The Thing, taken unawares, was drenched. A minute before, he had undeniably been black, but when he shook and blinked and looked at himself, he had turned white.

"All right, joker," he snarled, "so you won that round."

The man turned about with a new look on his face. Central Park South towered serenely in the air. "Let's play for it," the man said. "Tallest building wins." "Agreed," said the Thing. He was shivering in spite of himself. The man stretched out his arms from Fifth to Central Park West, and brought them slowly together. The buildings came in softly like a pack of cards. He held the deck and the Thing drew. The man drew. The Thing showed; the Plaza. The man showed, and laughed. The Huntington Hartford Museum.

Of late a Thing lurches through the Park, harmless and errant as a disincarnate shadow. It walks only at night, when it feels safe from marauders—children, nurses, sunlight, Good Humor men. It has something on its back; a pleasant homunculus with an unpressed look. The man likes to badger the Thing. "Just look at yourself," he says, "all hell, all history, and you can't win. You can't even pull a right card."

"All right, get off it," whines the Thing.

"Not yet," the man smiles. "Once more around the tow path. I need exercise. Let's go."

They get going.

THE EDGE

An old man I knew used to roller-skate in Central Park.

Wheels! he'd shout. Wheels!—That's the shape of the future. I've even got them in my head. Come here!

And sure enough, when he tipped his head you could hear that sound, like a sea in a shell, a steady hum of wheels on hard wood, a skate-athon.

Walkers! Why, you people jerk along like puppets on wires. The old man guffawed. Walking! "A series of frustrated falls." Well, go ahead, be frustrated. They ought to put you strollers on film; you'd look about as graceful as a cut from the Great Train Robbery.

His wife had skated too. She was dead long ago.

What a trooper she was, he said. (A gleam of memory, no grief.) She died on her feet. We were doing an eight day job together, linked arms, figures and all. I thought her hands were getting chilly toward the end. But I pulled her to the finish, dead on her feet. We came in third. Pinned the medal on her, before they closed the box. Bronze. I let her have it. Gold medal, I'd have thought twice.

When I was younger! I used to pick up speed, turn a cartwheel on skates and come down with a crack like a

whip. I bet everything I had. I won every time. I'd even
come down on the same length of board I'd taken off
from. You could have shot an arrow or drawn a plumb
line between where I landed, where I'd taken off.

What would I like to do? Just ask me! Skate to the
edge of the world and look over! Bet the Greeks were
right, it's shaped like a pie plate. I'd like to see what
God looks like. Does he make the pie, or eat it, or both?
Why, I'd like to do the whole damned thing, cartwheel-
ing over all the silly frontiers; let all that fool's straw—
marks, francs, pounds, pesos, visas—fall out of my
pockets. I'd have my underwear painted like a circus and
let it go, a big flag running down a pole like a monkey.

I haven't done it all yet. When you do it all, you race
north and meet someone racing south. My old opposite
number, death on wheels. I've beat him before, I could
do it again. What a collision that'd be, at the speed
I make! (He pushed his chest out like a pigeon.) I'd
pull him in like a rag doll or a boned chicken. I'd get
the old bird to the finish line. Why, he'd win with me;
or come in second at least—way above his average!

He skated off with a flourish, his grin stood in the air.
He would, too.

THE FIRST DAYS OF THE SCIENCE
OF PRENATAL COMMUNICATION

THERE WAS ONCE a child who even before birth caused his parents profound trouble of mind. It had been a peaceable, normal pregnancy, but in the seventh month the mother began to undergo a series of unsettling experiences. From time to time, she heard the child's heartbeat as a kind of high irregular beep. At first, she comforted herself with the thought that any offspring of hers was bound to be highly strung. After all, she said to herself, we're space people; Daddy's work at Rand is bound to show.

But she gradually grew aware of a pattern that faulted her optimism. The beeps were audible only from nine to five during the day. Moreover they repeated themselves according to an intricate pattern of long and short. She took the sounds down on paper, and went to her husband.

He was instantly excited. I'm certain it's a message, he exulted. I'll take it to our code people.

The Rand team confirmed it beyond any doubt. In ten hours they had broken the code. Under secrecy, the parents were handed a transcription. The child was saying; get me an outside line, or failing that, get me out of here.

The code team, in fact the whole corporation, was delighted beyond measure. They set up an intricate cybernetic complex, involving extrasensory perception, and began to talk of a new science, prenatal communication.

Messages began to pass regularly between the world and the unborn child. In the week that followed, four were transcribed. They included an inquiry relating to moon photos taken by the Russians, a request in slightly cooler tones that his mother control her Martini intake, a marked expression of dislike for the family dog, and a complaint against an acrimonious family quarrel which, he said, had interrupted his reflections. If his father could not keep his voice down, his mother must.

But such episodes were momentary ripples in a still pond. Nature was conspiring gently toward this extraordinary birth; public interest was in a fever. It was decided that the child would be born in a specially prepared room at Rand. And in order to include the world in an unprecedented moment, the President of the United States would exchange greetings with the parents and the newborn child, via telstar. Moreover, several universities had offered doctoral scholarships to the child, to be pursued at its own pace and discretion. The child (by now it was apparent that it was a boy) conveyed its satisfaction with these arrangements.

So the child matured. One day toward the end of the ninth month, he asked to have read to it Blake's *Jerusalem*, and the *Letters* of Madame Blavatsky. That same evening, the mother felt a peculiar lassitude come over her, a floating lightness of spirit. All her fears vanished. She sat alone on a balcony of the apartment overlooking the East River, where the tugs and steamers rode the twilight waters, scattering the stars in their wake.

She slept, and her dream was terrible.

Her waking landscape was unchanged. But the air was charged with malignancy and woe. Her child rode through the night astride a horse. Once, then a second time, a third, and yet a fourth, he crossed her vision. The horse he rode was alight with a devouring apocalyptic blaze.

War, he trumpeted, war over the world. A second time he passed. Famine, they shrieked, child and horse together. A third vision; the terrible cry was, Plague, Plague! Then a fourth—. But the mother rose in her chair and fell like a stone to the floor.

A few hours later, the child was born dead.

PRAY TOGETHER — STAY TOGETHER

THE FAMILY KATZENBAUEN was famous throughout seventeenth century Bavaria. They displayed to all the nation a precious example: fidelity, affection, faith, discipline.

But there was more. The Katzenbauens were a circus family. They had developed over the years a truly astonishing feat of resolution, symmetry and daring. It went like this. As the band played, the father, mother, three sisters and three brothers, dressed in matching lederhosen, skirts and blouses, would step forward into the ring. Then on signal, in perfect timing, the oldest son would leap to his father's shoulders, the next to his, then the next; the mother would follow, then the elder sister, and so on up. Finally, like a climbing star, a golden haired little girl would miraculously appear on the topmost rung of this living ladder, this line of life and strength and harmony. The sight brought the crowds to their feet again and again, in a spontaneous tribute of adoring joy. Our family! The crown of the fatherland!

But that was not all, there was a further climax. The throngs settled down again, the last note of the glockenspiel and drum died away. The lights dimmed. Then came the moment, always awaited, always new. From

bodice and pocket, each of the Katzenbauens drew a
card. The message flashed through the darkness, "The
family that prays together stays together!" The words
held for a long breathless moment, and then dissolved.
The lights went on, the band flourished, the Katzenbauens stood shoulder to shoulder in the ring, their hands
joined, bowing and flushed and triumphant.

The perfection of their act had of course exacted
years of practice. And practice remained essential, lest
the edge wear off its surprise and daring. So the family
retired periodically to the high Alps, where papa Katzenbauen would bring his flock for a holiday. There on
the heights, it seemed as though all nature joined in
the message of fidelity and unity; pray together, stay together! From time to time, together in the high bloom-
studded pastures, their joy would quite overcome them.
They would leap, singing, spontaneous, to one another's
shoulders, with no audience save the birds and the high
clear heavens. To pray together, to stay together! An
entreaty which the gods themselves could not but favor.

One day, the gods could no longer refuse. The day
was perfect, all nature rejoiced. In twin mirrors of earth
and heaven, shone the perfect face of noon. As though
in response to a law of their being, the Katzenbauens
leaped joyously into formation. The golden child
mounted her father and mother and brothers and sisters,
a noonday star; the line of life stood taut as a guywire.
Then, without warning, as the family stood and
prayed, together and together, it thundered on the left.
The line shuddered and held, its ecstasy unsundered;
hands clasped to thighs, life held to life in a grasp of
stone.

The thunder rolled away, its echoes followed. The

family stood, like a single being. The sun faltered imperceptibly in its brightness; the family stood, as one man stands, lost in thought or thoughtlessness. The light receded. The shadow of the family lengthened, as though its life were draining away upon the earth. Evening came on, the Katzenbauens seemed turned to stone. The father stood, his great legs planted like pillars, his arms bent upward, crooked at the elbow, grasping in their terrible will all that life, all that unseen love, bulking upon him like time's thousand weight. The sons stood one on another, like lesser prophets on the shoulders of the great, seeing further, but comprehending less. The daughters stood; less weighty, more serene and tragic, remote, stricken with virginity, strangers to a fallen earth.

After 300 years they stand as they stood that noon. Only now, the father's feet are lost in the shifting earth, his shoulders are flaked and stony and thickened, his mouth drawn together like a frog's, his whole being a frowning icon, a father who stands for fatherland.

Together, they form a totem of stone upon that mountain plain, a forbidding prehistory of sorrow and waste. Few know their story; where it is known—the cries of triumph, the crowds, the adulation—the story is dismissed by rational men, who nevertheless have worn a path the long way round this dreadful presence. No prince has come to kiss and climb and kiss their curse into life. They pray, they abide, together and together.

THE YOUNG SHEPHERD

THERE WAS ONCE a young shepherd whom the people of the countryside used to call the good shepherd.

Good—why, he's as good as gold, they would insist with emotion. You have only to watch him—absolutely devoted. He'll go barefoot over stones to get a lamb out of the brambles, he sits up all night caring for a sick ewe. He knows a hundred sheep by name, at the least. And who can match him at shearing time, or in training the dogs to be as canny and gentle as himself? What a way the man has with dumb beasts!

They would go on and on like this. People who were ordinarily grudging and sour of mind, and had little to say in praise of anyone, could be turned on like spring runnels when his name came up.

The shepherd, however, took all this with a grain of salt. He remained silent, he was not taken in. Indeed, he had a wider knowledge of the world than a sheepfold could afford a man. He had lived abroad for many years, had come back to the mountain village after mysterious and tragic times—prison and torture, it was said, at the hands of men who had best remain nameless. Sometimes indeed, one sensed the village talk about his shining virtue was a way of avoiding issues. There were dark things in the village past, the talk smelled of evasion.

But what of him? He seemed remote and austere, as though his life belonged to another land, another time. It was not only that suffering had left its mark on him, in the most literal sense. There was something else—a cicatrice of the soul, other voices sounding in his ears, other griefs, larger beckonings.

A shepherd? He despised his people's ideal. If he played their role, it was only for a price. The price was a respite, the peace necessary before he could grow another skin and step out of their world, and disappear. Disappear, as their ideal shepherd, that is, and forever. Indeed, how else could he bring them to see that they were hiding out in a sheepfold, because he and the dogs were on guard, on call? That was the duplicity that corrupted their charade. Insincerity, self-love, insolvency of heart! They could be neutral and passive, because he was good. They were sheep because he was shepherd. He was their prize exhibit of the canton; shearer, midwife, bolus, emetic, victim, medicine man.

They had buried the truth under years of dread. He lay in a grave heaped with rotten flowers, the lies they were living, the lie that killed. He had come through, and stood again, after the tempest. But what of them?

It tortured him, the role they cast upon him like a foul pelt, tied cunningly at the waist, fitted out with head and hands. He looked out unblinkingly from sheep's eyes, he spoke their tongue, he stank of the herd. He was dipped and branded; our Savior, we are his people . . .

One day, a day like all the rest, when the village arose

to feed, to follow the sun and lie down again, that day which was like all the other days, he decided to end the act. He would disappear. It was as simple as that.

And so he did. He walked out on them, while the stars were fading, and the village lay innocent and somnolent under the moon. The god who was their god, a god of sheep, was no more. He disappeared into the world.

Inquiries were made of course, with great discretion. Men could not afford to raise a stir beyond the village boundary. It would not do to have old wounds opened, good reputations blasted. It was better to be denied even a good thing, if the cost of its recovery was too high; so the village council agreed. His work was taken over by others.

If hirelings botched the job, if illness and neglect and loss struck the flock, these too were borne with. Life must go on.

But what of him? Of his fate, of the people he settled among, and of the work he founded, nothing was heard. His mother had always been a silent woman; after his departure she spoke no more, she was hardly seen again. She entered a tragic doorway in the side of a hill, and walked through, and the door closed.

The tributes paid her memory had an air of both regret and relief. His face, as it had lived on in hers, his glance, softened and blurred, but unmistakably present in hers, vanished from sight and mind. It was better after all to be rid of such presences, such reminders—of sorrow, of sin, of atonement unpaid.

They took up her corpse with a sigh, a burden that exacted silence and a march in unison. They bore her body to its rest, they lowered it in its grave. No more of

him, no more of her. The burden of greatness was light-
ened; men could straighten their shoulders and be men
once more; which is to say, desperate, small of mind
and tongue, conniving, fearful. But still, but still—free.

The very hills folded in with a sigh; struck once with
a fist, cursed with human shape and voice and destiny,
nature became itself again, with a long suspiration of
relief. Somnolent and myth-ridden, the cycle began
anew.

THE ZOO KEEPER

THERE WAS ONCE a minor prophet among an ancient people. He died young, but not before there welled up in him a consuming sense of loss, a sense of being cheated of something. But of what? he pondered and pondered, as his travail approached.

His own people had condemned him. But he was not entirely bereft of consolation; he knew that sour grapes set teeth on edge. He knew also that a man must endure his times and that his own times were undoubtedly evil. Still he was eaten by loss, he carried a fox at his heart. Time, time, he needed time! And time was being denied him, and where lay his recourse?

A packed tribunal had convicted him of atheism. He had turned away from the state deities. He accepted the judgment; with regard to their gods, he was indeed an unbeliever, beyond hope of conversion.

But at length even the slight consolation afforded by his upright life, drained from his soul. He was left with a sick regret—for life denied, for knowledge withheld, for cheated years. He was indeed a stranger upon the earth, he knew little of his own country, he was ignorant and unknown—and he must die.

And what rumors he had heard of the great world and

of animals weird in form, bizarre in color, dazzling in variety, beyond the horizon to east and west. What marvels was the world holding out—forever beyond his reach? The torture was that he would never know.

Just before the blade descended, he made a great pact with the Almighty. With a final twist of his body and spirit, he willed to be reborn, in another century. Whether he would ever again pour blood on the altar or unroll the scriptures, was a matter of indifference. What counted was that he might some day burst the membrane of his ignorance and see the world. He might ride a camel and hear the honk of geese, and see for himself whether a curious animal, as he had been told, slept upside down, like a hive on tendrils. . . .

He works today in Central Park Zoo, a keeper of beasts. In the midst of a people who have seized command of their world, who are powerful and purposeful and unconscionably arrogant, he serves the captive beasts. The Park is aflow with a great stream of life; on both banks the enormous catacombs of the living are raised and pulled down again; exotic, absurd, electric with life. In the midst of the park, like a ghetto under lock and key, is the zoo; within, he, its minor functionary. Indifferent and archaic, he hews wood and draws water, a slave among beasts.

The images which illumine his existence are drawn from the earth, from hooves and pelts. He smells the urine-soaked straw, he sees himself in the bestial faces. The setting of his life, mocking and pretentious, glitters in the mirror of the Park lake. Vanity of vanities—a city seen in water.

Day after day, the great avenues ring like a corps of drummers, with the fantastic heartbeat of this people.

Peace, they drum, war, they crash. Equality, property, human rights, human wrongs. Men march past, their faces lit with holy or infernal passion. And the beasts look up, distracted for a moment, and turn once more to their bran and water. He feeds them water and bran, and rakes their dung in heaps, and carts it away, a lesser keeper in a minor zoo.

One night in spring, after some years of this existence, he sat at the edge of the pool where the sea lions swam and fed and crept ashore. The bronze beasts in the clock had rounded the midnight circuit with their drums and flutes, the lovers had departed, the lights went out. The life that pulsed around him lay heavy on the air. Forsythia, magnolia, cherry and apple, the forest growth of a parasitic city.

He drank the draught of the spring night, its bitterness poured into his soul. He was lonely and cold and numb; his life was a great cry of the heart, a protest against the course of his existence. He knew that the stars were liars, that his passion had betrayed him. He was trapped in a zoo, a captive playground. He was part of an inexorable defeat; one with the innocent, the baited, the victim. *Homo captus*, the sign on his paling read—"Captive Man." All the day long, all the night long, I have lifted my voice to a blind and unheeding people. God would become man, the old oracles said. But must man become a beast?

The morning star arose above him, unutterably pure and serene. The animals stirred and arose where they slept. He lifted his eyes to another day. Where there was no joy, hope must suffice.

DAY OF JUDGMENT

THERE WAS ONCE a land owner, mortgage holder, tax collector, and used-car dealer. He died, and was welcomed into Abraham's bosom.

Dives was, to say the least, astounded. I was prepared, he murmured to himself with a smile, for a different outcome. Were the prophets wrong, and the law, and the oracles, and Jesus; not to speak of Confucius and the warnings of my wife?

He was ushered into a dining hall as vulgar as the one from which he had recently and in some disarray, been borne. He sat down to his interrupted meal; his guts awakened like a suckling at the dugs. . . .

On the same day, a poor man also died. His death came like a vast yawn of release; Dives had held mortgages on all his possessions; his house, car, and land; indeed his very body was enslaved. He died, and was buried in hell.

Lazarus was appalled. Have I lived my eighty righteous years in vain? I was one of the poor men lauded in the psalms, churchgoers envied me, nuns and priests assured me I was on the right path.

He sank down feebly on a dung heap; it was as noisome as the one he had occupied for so long on earth. Above

47

him, a palace doorway loomed, familiar and depressing.
He had no need to glance up. He knew its coat of arms
by heart; a bowl of truffles and caviar, a crossed knife and
fork, the words; *venter vincit omnia.* The gate was of
course bolted.

The arrival of the two men reverberated through hell
and heaven.

In heaven, where more freedom prevailed, pickets appeared before official buildings; they chanted, Lazarus,
yes; Dives, no. Authorities were shaken. They're not going
to make a theological Joan of Arc out of me, God fumed
to his wife. If they start marching around here, the
police will know what to do.

The devil faced a similar unrest, though it had different overtones. He was assailed with subtle provocations
of mockery. A series of anonymous letters reached him,
raising questions of his virility, his competence, the
loyalty of the army. Was he not perhaps growing senile?
Was it not time for a referendum? One morning, along
his garden wall, there appeared two blunt words in white
lead paint, hard to erase; Powerlessness corrupts.

Thus the fate of poor man and rich, badly handled in
the estimate of their peers, raised a growing storm. Times
were changing, foundations were shaken. By way of pride
and expediency and desperation, the authorities under-
took various projects. In heaven, the tax on incomes was
raised; in hell, an anti-poverty program was voted. To no
avail. The civil troubles continued and grew.

It was not revealed how a solution came about. But
one morning, a scene unparalleled in the history of both
countries took place. At the guarded frontier which sep-
arates heaven and hell, two vehicles appeared just before
dawn. From a farm wagon drawn by an old dray horse,

an enormous figure lowered itself to the ground. The gate was lowered, the fat man advanced. Behind, a procession of porters made their way, burdened with trunks and bundles. The customs men checked their lists; fifty suits of clothing, quatrocento paintings, gold bullion in quantity, classical recordings, a bulky folder of securities. A passport was checked. It was valid for passage; it declared the bearer immune from yellow fever and gonorrhea. Dives passed through the barricade into hell.

Meantime, from a limousine on the other side, long as a gangster's hearse, an aged crotchety man emerged. He came forward alone. He carried only a stick, weighted at one end with a bundle. The guards opened his possessions, and hailed him through.

The fat man climbed into the Mercedes Benz, the motor tuned up, whining softly. It turned its nose and went off, gently as a fish, into the liquid dawn.

On the other side, Lazarus mounted the wagon. The old horse, startled into wakefulness, twisted about in his creaking shafts. The cart jerked into motion; and moved off.

In ten minutes, the border was once more normalized.

THE BOX

I KNEW A GIRL who carried a box around with her. She used to say with a sigh—It's my only world, a square world.

Once we were sitting on a park bench, in May. She opened the box with a grimace and pulled out, one after another, a worm that walked, a fish that smiled when tickled, a barnacle with a flea on its stomach, a sloth recovering from a nervous breakdown.

What a world, she sighed.

It's beautiful, I said.

Take your choice, she said, it's all up for grabs.

I don't know, I thought.

She said, Anything you take, it spells trouble.

I said, You're a strange one, so young and so hopeless.

Who's young? she objected. Haven't you ever heard of Pandora? I've been around New York a long time. All my friends say, Her name's Pandora. Take something from her square box, you'll regret it.

Never mind, I said, I buy it. How about if I take the whole bit?

You mean it? she said, her face lighting up like a window. You mean you'll take the whole ape off my back?

It's not the ape I want, I came out with, it's you. Don't you see, you beautiful mournful ninny? I love you.

It was the weirdest moment in the history of the island. She broke down crying. Her silly animals sat up in their box, ugly and intent as eagles in a nest, all eyes and appetite, eating our words alive. When I said, I love you, I swear I heard them flap their wings. And when she said something inane like, I love you, too, they flew straight into her eyes like cuckoos into a clock.

The box snapped shut like a demented trap, gave a puff of soot and vanished.

Love, she says to me every day; Love, you did it all, my bad dream's gone.

But I say—No, Love, it's like bed and board. Some things you can only do together.

HOPE, OR ALL IS NOT LOST
BUT ALMOST ALL

A CHILD ONCE APPEARED in New York, clothed only in a green ribbon draped across its hips. On the ribbon was spelled in big mortician letters of gold, E P O H.

One autumn day in late afternoon, the child was wandering alone on Park Avenue. It is a tribute to the enormous sangfroid of New Yorkers that her appearance caused no perceptible reaction. She seemed withdrawn, she moved according to some inner whim, now at a light run, now in a kind of slow trance.

Given the foot traffic and the time of day, the predictable occurred. The child chose, near a certain crowded spot on the corner of Eightieth Street, to break into a lope. Directly in her course, a lady in mink was absorbed in managing the leashes of a dalmatian and a toy poodle. Somewhat like a rope skipper who has missed her entrance cue, the child ran head on into the trio. The resultant confusion was considerable. The matron was upended, her outcries were vehement, so it was not immediately evident that she was also unharmed. Anger led to moral outrage; charges were brought, and the child, now surrounded by considerable public interest, was borne off to the police station.

There, she proved unresponsive as a stone. When asked her name, her domicile, the reason for her singular attire, she answered nothing. She stood there limp as a landed fish, objecting to nothing, volunteering nothing. Finally, after some delay and considerable tumult, the charges were announced. Given the age and condition of the defendant, they may have seemed excessive. They were vagrancy and contempt of court.

It was only then, astonishingly enough, as the child was being led away, that by some circumstance or other, a fact dawned on someone. The child had a name; she was called H O P E, a backward name at best. On the green ribbon which clothed her like an inadequate gift wrapping, the word had indeed been spelled backward. She was H O P E; moreover, she was deaf, dumb and blind.

Having ventured on an absurd episode, let us see it through to its illogical outcome. The year, let us say, is 1890. The child, of whom we have no further intelligence, dies in prison, like a Dickens heroine, too virtuous for the real world, too absurdly good to redeem a bad novel.

Still, she cannot be entirely disposed of; she lives on, a question, an unease in the mind. Does her fate, her condemnation, repeated under various circumstances even to this day, hold some meaning for the judge, for the dalmatian, for the obscure person whose outrage triggered the child's fate, indeed, for the human bloodline? We do not know. The curtain rings down, the audience disperses, filled with a sense of obscure failure, diffuse as twilight on a day which has seen no sun. We can perhaps accept it that we are the merest bystanders at a drama whose cost we are never summoned to pay, though its outcome is crucial to our existence. We can accept it that a child

named H O P E should endure her ordeal without us,
who are cast nonetheless by the course of her tragedy,
into a pit of loss—without her, without means of endur-
ance or escape. We can perhaps accept it that H O P E
is without succor, is illiterate (or more properly blind),
that she stands under the rigor of the law.

For we are, if not skilled in the uses of failure, at least
able to parry its blows. We will survive; the arguments in
our favor are before us, visible, grandiose, persuasive; our
city, our sleek dogs and their furred owners, our police,
our public order, our souls. Shall we not win through,
hopeless as we are, surrounded by the corrupt surrogates
of our innocence lost, pawned away, put to death?

THE STATUE

ONCE IN A remote Indian town, after many years of faithful service, a guru finally attained the first place in the temple priesthood. The price of his new honor was a severe one. He had passed exhausting years devoted to training young monks, to copying texts and supervising festival arrangements. But now his duties were radically reduced. An honorific and, if truth were admitted, somewhat boring routine remained to him.

It came down to this. Once a week, with a silver mounted brush, a golden scissors as long as his arm, and a quantity of bee's wax, he entered the triple court, passed through the damask curtain, and stood at length before the enormous feet of the god. Then his task would begin; he cut and shined the toenails of the great image.

The statue had a tumultuous history. Its trunk and head had been lost. They had toppled in some former aeon; not a trace of the upper members remained. But from knees to instep, the stone colossus stood, the chief treasure of the people, their god among men. The enormous broken knees, covered with a trace of drapery, jutted through the open roof, cubits above the head of priest and people.

55

It is not superfluous to record, surely, that the priest was witness to a miracle which never ceased to move his heart. The toenails, of the god that is, grew; they grew approximately an inch every week. And though the broken image was of stone, it was undeniable that the toenails were of some other substance, entirely mysterious and beautiful, their surface glittering like mica, their depths milky as mother-of-pearl.

The nail clippings he carefully gathered up week by week, and distributed to the faithful.

Now on a certain Sunday, the priest finished his stint as usual. It had required no more than a half hour. He had clipped the nails and filed their edges, spread a coating of wax on the toes of the image, rubbed them with a chamois cloth until they glowed like black phosphor. He paused for a long moment, bowed profoundly before the image, then turned and started out of the holies, his silver box of clippings under his arm, his tools in hand.

A familiar sense of depression welled up in him as he traversed the three courts. What the hell, he thought to himself with a sigh, back to the plateau of the middle forties. A glorified shoe shine with retirement benefits. That god! One half hour of work a week; and I don't even know if he exists. Who does know? Who ever heard of a god from the knees down?

Clearly, a crisis of faith was brewing. He could see less and less point, he said to himself with growing conviction, to play wet nurse to a heap of dry bones.

Yet his depression remained inventive. Like a mariner in a gale, he kept a weather eye out in all directions, for any change that might bring him advantage, for a new sky, or a new tack in the wind.

He was even inclined to pray at times, as the temple manual urged. Nothing happened for better or worse. But since his hopes were not high, he was not greatly cast down.

Why indeed this trouble of mind? He wished he could know. Sometimes he sensed obscurely that the wish was father to the act; that he did know, that the truth was pushing and nudging at his shoulder with a finger of stone, a lost finger of a lost arm of a lost body . . . Was he not universally respected, had he not come into possession of a sinecure many coveted and none held but he? Yes, yes, yes. The finger jabbed, a tic in his very soul. Yes, but he was dying, petrifying, in the service of a dead god.

One night he slept, and while he slept, a dream came to him. It seemed that he stood in the temple, on the pedestal of his new honor; and while he stood there, he glanced down. Then, precisely as though awaiting his glance, out of a curtained embrasure, a man no larger than an insect scuttled to his feet, took up an enormous ritual scissors, and began to cut his toenails. The priest stood there, invisible, remote, bathed in a kind of obscene stupefaction. Suddenly, a cry of triumph or despair from his servitor drew his attention once more. The little man had paused in his task; his form arched upward, like a gladiator in victory; he held up for trophy, a great bleeding toe; the toe of Goliath or Holofernes. Then as the priest cried aloud in anguish and rage and realization, he heard the little man at his feet yell: wake up! wake up!

He awakened, bolt upright, bathed in sweat. His little son was shaking him by the shoulders.

MADAME ZERO

MADAME ZERO WAS by common agreement, a marvel. She told fortunes in a walkup on Third Avenue, an area uniquely suited to Madame's style, which was both timeless and anonymous. There, under her Spartan gaze, almost as though by her sufferance, the brownstones and pubs and thrift shops awaited the hammer and the ghostly high rise.

Not the least of Madame's attractions was her staggering honesty. It was so transparent that her clients almost never thought to be grateful for it. Or perhaps another quality outshone even her integrity; the fact was that Madame was never, never wrong.

If she saw that an unborn child would be produced cross-eyed or pigeon-toed, she said so. And the child was. If you were to die that year, she told you so, and you did.

But Madame was no doomsday star. Which is to say, she plied her trade about the way life does, half foul, half fair. One client came into money, another encountered a beautiful girl and won her, a sick relative of another came 'round. Sometimes things went swimmingly—for some. Madame sat there, remote from fortune and mischance, dealing her cards, telling it as it was; she was impartial as a pendulum, clairvoyant and blind, compassionate and merciless.

Indeed, it could not be denied, Madame was a fascinator. She would breathe on the crystal, belch, draw forward, reach into time's murky waters, and grab—tomorrow! Slippery as a prawn. She'd pull it out, hold it up for you to see. See? she'd face you, unblinking. And she never got older. It was uncanny.

One day she was sitting there as usual, boneless and black as a scampi, eyes half closed in the half light. One client had just left, another was coming in the door. The two settled down, facing one another across the battered table; antagonists, lovers. The room they sat in was stale and dirty as a cage.

Madame, as usual, wasted no words. Greetings? The fates do not greet a man, they dispose of him. Madame reached for her ball and drew it toward her. She bent forward, raised her arm like a trawling tool—and suddenly stiffened.

She had seen something, she had been seen. Her arm dropped to the table, nerveless, wooden. Then she screamed aloud. It was as though a hand had grasped her, she fought like a fish, her eyes stood like death.

Then she was gone, once and for all. It was as simple, as terrible as that, as though a net had whooshed through the air, pulled her out of sight and mind.

Third Avenue, broad daylight. What had occurred, among the vegetables and vendors, the varicose faces? Had Madame been grasped, the dark formless baggage of someone else's vision? Did she squirm somewhere, a fish in a fist, held before some mysterious client, his good or evil news, his long lost, his death or birth, his change of luck?

Turn about is fair. We never knew, we will never know.

CRXXSS

THE BOAT

THERE WAS ONCE a giraffe named Mordecai. He had a friend with a spade beard and a long nose and coat. The two used to meet every afternoon at the fence paling of a zoo and stand there, hours on end.

Neither could speak. Divine providence had never told why. Both had protective coloration. It was quite evident why.

The Jew had been born in a grave, during a pogrom. His parents were little addicted to speech, even in the corners where they passed the larger part of their existence. Their life was indeed a curiosity. Their daring to meet, to fall in love, was an affront. They paid for the crime shortly after the birth of their child, by disappearing.

The giraffe had been born in protective custody, of a hot coupling by two animals who were, like himself, mute. His parents ran like clouds, and made thunder with their hooves.

The Jew, forbidden many areas of human life, came to love the giraffe, because he seemed harmless as a cloud, because he was long of neck and of spotted pie, because his existence, his captivity, his silence, all seemed to speak of a providential collusion in nature.

Within certain limits, the giraffe ran where he listed, as the scripture said. Indeed, he seemed a scriptural invention; his long neck was top-heavy as a flower on a thin stem. He was innocent of all malice, a curiosity; like a child's animal, he seemed to contain nothing but air.

Air, that was it. They could travel together. The man of the long coat leaped the fence and sat down astride the giraffe. Then the animal gathered speed and left the Earth. They rode the heavens together, the man clutching a mandolin, a rose twined in his beard. They raced over a little town on a crisp spring evening. A fat milkmaid and her cow looked aloft in astonishment.

The two were making for another flying object. Miles and years ahead, lost in the firmament, a man stood impaled on a tree, naked but for a clout; it was inscribed with Jewish characters that went off and on in green and red. In red, the sign was *House of Josue*. In green, it was *Look up and live*.

It was quite a convention. The sky curved like an ark, toward them, away from them. Josue came in like a sea bird and planted himself amid decks like a mainsail. Then Mordecai and his friend landed softly. Below decks, there was mewing, hissing, flapping, groaning, roaring, chomping; all of it distant and gentle, as though uttered in sleep and heard in sleep.

They sailed on without haven or harbor, an ark of animals and humans, their moorings cut loose by a rabbi's knife. O the circumcized hearts, the tinkers, the harpers, the lovers, the tellers of tales, the publicans, the weavers, the makers of pottery! The poor were fed, the blind saw, the lame men leapt like David. All the animals wore yamulkas; days they composed psalms by free asso-

ciation, nights they made love. And God spoke to them
out of the whirlwind, hot as a lover in the act of love,
hating them, bearing down hard. O the tempests. Not
easy, not easy it was, the course of the wandering Jew
boat, filled to brim like a napkin of creation. Thank
you Mister Chagall.

FAIRY TALE

THERE IS A hankering in your heart, the holy man said, whose intensity grows as the years pass; to enjoy a modest, peaceable, rational life. Such an existence (if I may be allowed to envision it for you) is a marriage between sweet reasonableness within and reasonable men without.

Alas. I have news for you. The marriage exists only in the fond ruminations of aging parents. Locked chastely in one another's arms, they dream toward dawn that in some impregnable keep, safe from time and dragons, their daughter is locked in the arms of her spouse; they lie there dreaming that their daughter, in a castle keep, etc.

A mirror game, you see (he spread his hands) with time reduced to a fairy tale consistence, tamed, devoid of all bone and marrow.

Whereas, in real time, the story of man is a tale told by a certain—was it Berber?

Perhaps it was Thurber? the man corrected gently.

Yes. (The holy man arose.) In any case, read it once again before tomorrow's session: *The Night the Bed Fell In.*

THE BIRD

Q<small>UITE POSSIBLY WE</small> are the only creatures who do so many things so well, a bird said airily to a man. Why, look at the record: we breed in unlikely places, we grow gorgeous plumage, we fly with utmost grace, we nest in a thousand daring ways; and all this with no help from you.

No wonder Lao Tsi was in wonderment at us. We have always fascinated your wise men, we are the specks in the pure crystal of their minds, the fault in their excellence that drives them on to a further effort, a further sky.

As for the gospel, who but we have understood what the Lord was driving at? Which of you has taken Him at His word, as we have? Who loves the poor as we do? who brings them joy? You'll find us singing in hut doorways, all around the world. And wasn't it Someone of import who commended ornithology to your attention, urging you to "consider the birds of the air?" He knew our secret; don't sow or reap or plan or exterminate or grow rich or think of tomorrow. Where's tomorrow, anyway, when the weather changes? A thousand miles to the south.

O we know how to travel, too. I seem to recall (he

cocked his head) "take with you neither scrip nor staff."
When you think of it, we're really among the last
Christians around. When the sun is out, we sing. When
the grain is in tassel, we're like Ruth, living off your
surplus.

Well, the man said lamely, you don't leave us much.
And at least you admit we leave you something. . . .

Yes, the bird said—and we leave you something, too.
We love what you love, when all's said. We nest in your
statues, in the generals' pockets and muskets and the
horses' iron manes. That's easy; thanks for the public
convenience. But we will be really reconciled to having
you around, when a few of you learn—

Learn what? The man was eager now. It had cost too
much, he had come too far, to lose the ending.

Learn your own gospel. Learn to love. I know it
sounds easy. It may sound useless, even. Quite possibly
it is. But everything you've put your money on, for so
long, is far more useless. When you plot and connive
and tantalize and wave big sticks and beat the bushes—
the birds vanish. And so may you. It comes down to
this: we can only take you (he was getting serious, a
child prodigy) when you decide to take one another.
Is that easy? I could play dodo and say—from a stuffed
mouth—of course, it's easy. Or—yes, it's absurd.

But all I can say—on the wing—is: it's possible.
Come on!

THE DREAM

A BANK EXECUTIVE once had a dream whose early
stages sent a wave of warmth coursing through his ample
frame. It seemed that a large number of major and
minor functionaries, accountants, investors, brokers, im-
porters, exporters, purveyors, surveyors and advisors,
had gathered to do him honor in a midtown hotel ball-
room. The speeches were satisfactory. In and out of the
dream, acts and audiences, he found himself tapping
his coverlet, counting the American Beauty roses, and
taking notes on his napkin. Entirely befitting, he mut-
tered as the tributes swelled, entirely right—if somewhat
overlong. In his own office, surrounded by his lackeys, he
would long ago have put his foot against a buzzer under
the rug, calling a halt to the proceedings. But patience,
he admonished himself, as a sweating myrmidon led him
for the sixth time down glory road. Patience. *Noblesse
oblige.*

The speaker finished. The lights dimmed. Across the
room, as though borne on the cresting surf of applause,
a vehicle of Venus, a serving cart rolled. It was alight
with a great confection, a triumph of the baker's art. The
cake was shaped like a bank vault; behind windows of

rock candy, the silver doors gleamed and smiled. Be like us, they urged. Be safe, the rust enters not.

He cut the cake. Inside in a large hollow space, there lay a silver tool, a file. He took it up, amused. Attached by a string was a message. He read it, as he supposed, aloud. His voice fell like a news of death, of calamitous truth, upon a thoughtless scene. He said simply, as though to himself, a detached and ignorant reveler: HELP IS AT HAND.

ONE MAN

Once, only one man existed.

There was nothing to measure him against.

No one to say how tall he stood, what was his complexion, why he walked upright.

Yet he stood up from the earth and made a shadow.

Or he lay down at night; and always, the earth was against his feet or his whole length.

He was industrious; he learned to read.

And he made himself a rough image to do reverence to.

One day, touched by an obscure depression, he daubed himself with paint, and wrote on his thigh the word, *nothing*; on his groin, *nothing*; on his arm, *nothing*; on his forehead, *nothing*; on his two feet, *nothing*.

But the mood passed; good days returned.

On one of them, he washed in a river, and where he had written *nothing* and erased it, he wrote *God*; five times, *God*.

And then, again, erased that.

A contrary man.

Nothing was too little, God was too much.

Or betimes, his life regained its equilibrium; then his skin was a *tabula rasa*.

Once he read a story of a man's crime by Kafka; it

brought with it a weight both of anguish and of fresh inspiration; he would wound himself five times in the flesh.

At such a time, the word to be understood was: *guilty*.

Or again he made a crude kite and flew it; or stood erect under a waterfall.

Then, the word on his flesh was: *joy*; five-fold joy.

Now he is full of days.

The sum of his wisdom is in sky and waterfall and flesh: guilt, joy, God, nothing.

THE COMMUTER

A MIDDLE-AGED COMMUTER, content in his vocation, once passed a distressing night. An angel of the Lord, compassionate but unequivocal, and just under six feet in height, appeared to him in sleep. "Vanity of vanities," he intoned, "all is vanity." The commuter, whose vision was imperfect, was hazy as to who was being addressed. He looked distractedly over his left shoulder. His wife slept equably beside him.

The angel vanished with celerity. The man sank back on his pillow, and after a period of wakeful thought, slept until dawn.

He awakened to a commuter's day. His workaday spirit was neither depressed nor renewed. Indeed, the day began so precisely on schedule that it was only some half hour after awakening, as he was going downstairs to breakfast, that he recalled the ominous event of the night. And even then, it came to him only as a distraction comes to a man already launched on the main current of a day—a hesitation, a hint, a warning cloud across the sun. Nothing else. Necktie to laces, he was intact and mobile, his mind inviolate, his quality unassailed. He kissed his wife in the way of a fifty-year-old husband;

punctilio without passion. Their breakfast was pleasurable, as silent as the feeding of two fish.

Not even when he closed the front door, one half hour later, did he take warning. And then only slowly, in the way a man absorbs a series of repeated blows, and walks on carefully, and is struck again. He turned up the street toward the intersection and his bus stop. And there was nothing ahead.

Nothing, that is, but the scene he had just left. There stood his own house; green clapboard, thirty-two foot lawn, three evergreens, forsythia clump. And in the doorway, his wife turning away. He walked on, and in a most literal and terrifying sense, he got nowhere. There was his house again; to the right and left, ahead and behind; green clapboard, lawn, evergreens, forsythia; and his wife forever turning away in the door; a house of mirrors, a horror.

He walked and ran and slowed down. Nothing changed. He was forever coming on and passing by his own house, his own life. Some mocking hand was forever turning out the same lantern show; the film ran on and on, unsnarled, competent, mad; all was the same and the same under the sun, vanity and vanity. Any house was his, any world his own, forever and the same.

At length, he turned back precipitously and ran for it, he broke in and slammed the front door like a man who would hold out a deluge. And with the slam of the door, his world came to rest at length.

His wife was no sibyl. She was only a woman; but she excelled in the literacy test we name marriage. She could read an open book, she could discern in a face the mark of death or of birth, the onset of the angel. So,

not knowing what ailed him, she treated the distraught
man with calm and silence, a tact beyond praise.

He slept most of the day, feverish and unutterably
troubled. From the window, his neighbors' houses shone
in the sun. The children's voices rose in conflict and ex-
altation, the trees showed in the light a peacock glory, the
sun waxed and receded. He lay there like the dead, his
mind on fire. Tomorrow? he might once again rise to
what lay beyond; his street, his world, his nightmare?

TWO SOLDIERS

THERE WERE ONCE two young men of approximately the same age, sprung from vastly different soils of the earth.

They were thrown together by the centripetal force called modern war. Mars captured them alive in an open season, slammed their heads together with his mailed hands, and let them fall. Their bodies were taken up and buried with honor.

All but ignored in the fury which attended this event, was its meaning; the scope and freedom which Mars now enjoyed. Clearly, events were conspiring to create a new god, a new niche in the pantheon. Mars had plucked two men from their homelands, continents apart. He had armed them, aimed them at each other, given the signal —and buried the fallen. It was he who set the odds and took the bets; he finally, who hired the grave digger and guaranteed "perpetual care" for the noble dead.

Indeed, Mars had read the signs of the times; in order to survive in the twentieth century, a god must become not only a consummate technician, but a philosopher as well. He must deal not only with traditional matters of strategy, deployment, ordinance, and with rather more complex developments in technology. His real problem was an utterly new one; or rather, a very old one which the times were thrusting at him with a new urgency.

Who indeed was man?

The entrance of the war god into the ancient debate could not be indefinitely delayed. Generals, admirals, ministers of war, even soldiers could not hope for an honored place in a new world, while they stood mute before a question which was vexing thoughtful men everywhere. Should not the military be heard from, should it not lend to the question its prestige, its skill, its mythology, all it has learned in kindling and extinguishing the fires of the ages?

Indeed, Mars had something unique to offer. He knew what was in man. Moreover (and the point is not a frivolous one) he knew man as no one in the world could know him. He knew man standing in his bones, naked as an inductee, stripped of vanity and complexity.

And as this knowledge was sublimely simple, so was the method of gaining and communicating it. A darkened room, a pointer, an illuminated chart; three areas of the human frame: head, breast, belly. Man is a brain, a heart, a set of entrails. Three areas, three points of life where human blood converges and disperses again. And also, given the proper modes of entrance, three points of death.

To know man in his death! to know him in the act of dealing his death! To be skilled in the most exquisite, nervy and godlike acts, to render such acts socially honorable, to release their symbolism to the light of truth, to allow their divine afflatus to blow abroad. War, war alone could do this. And in so doing, war would perform the most useful and spiritual of functions; it would purify the blood of the tribe. Only in war do men hold to their lips again and again, like wine tasters in the cave of history, an ever more exquisite vintage of self knowledge, of moral passion. Raising the glass and announcing the toast, the soldier grows aware of who man is; in war he casts aside moral and historic fetters, asserts in his rapt vertical rigid form, like a caryatid of the universe, his responsibility toward the living and the dead, his angelic, transcendent quality, his ability to deal death with supreme discipline, a toreador before the horns, never to be turned aside by smells or sights which would destroy less febrile men . . . And finally, in war man toasts his gods; they are neither mutes nor blind men—nor eunuchs.

But we neglect our two soldiers.

They meet, let us fancy, after death. The setting is of no importance; we may imagine a deserted railway station just before dawn, a country place, a field or meadow above the sea, a battlefield transformed by time and art into an historic park.

It is important though, whatever the setting, that the young men appear in some way transfigured. Physically, they are entirely healed, agile. Their bodies have flowered; they bear a living point of glory where once their wounds were.

Their moral life is likewise transformed; they radiate inner light, peace, adroitness; they are serious, ironic, mature and thoughtful. As a consequence, it is unthinkable that their converse be tragic or grieving or weighted with memories of defeat.

These two have become at one stroke judges of the system that destroyed them. Death has plunged them deep in the stream of history, a total immersion. They are now baptized; they are become what they endured.

Their new life says *Credo* to all it once resisted, or partially accepted, or impurely welcomed.

Is it to be wondered then, that they speak like judges? Their persons hold something of the tense atrocious menace of a sword, bared but as yet unstained.

The fact is that Mars is hiding out from them.

One more note. We are free to think that in life, one of these soldiers was to the other as a shadow is to a grown man, toward the high noon of the day. But death, as the folklore of both their cultures reminds them, has equalized everything. Now it is almost as though——

—as though we drew on one another's death. I am smaller than formerly, you are larger. Though (sternly) I want it known I had nothing to do with your death!

—(mockingly) Nothing to do with my death? Nor I with yours?

—Correct. We were, as the record show, in different sectors when . . .

—Please. You miss my point. If I had nothing to do with your life, or you with mine, it follows that we had everything to do with one another's death.

—(smiling slowly) You've deepened. A philosopher! All hail! But tell me, does not your new insight stir your guts? Don't you long to do something with your new knowledge, as a man longs to try out a new weapon, a new idea, on the first life that comes along, whether it's a dog's or another man's?

—Well, yes. But in some project of worth, something life giving.

—That's a different sort of talk than the military is given to, or perhaps it is the same old talk; but your lips and tongue seem touched with a living coal. Has the truth touched us?

—Or is it that death has taken away our capacity for death? Is our biology renewed so that we can make love, as the pacifists said, instead of war?

—I used to love cast fishing, and I remember a great moment of my life—reeling in a five pound trout—such an arc of power and beauty that it seemed he was writing his own name, *rainbow*, as he leapt across the air.

—I remember something else. My guts blew up like a bladder fish, when the enemy went by. Even though he had not gone by. He was only being conjured up out of one of those old loudspeakers that came at you like a standing cobra.

—Still, it was not that we were killers; we hadn't enough sex or envy or cupidity for that. But the ideas in the air were killers; and they stung us first.

—Tell me, why did you enlist?

—Because it was normal. You did this thing with your body—as you had learned, from infancy, other uses for your other members. The enemy had not had the same advantages, and was still not housebroken. We were out to train him.

—(nodding) It was normal. One did not relish being a kook. There were no dropouts from the big net; I was landed too.

—But now I can understand the kooks better. They had found a shortcut to immortality; but one paid dearly for the secret; one had to be tried first, and found guilty. Was there not a saying somewhere—"we are made a spectacle . . ."?

—(impatiently) Yes, yes. But we're sitting here like old crones in rockers, sucking on our memories. Don't we disagree on anything any more?

—Perhaps. We don't know yet because we're waiting.

The real drama is beating away, like the heart I once
bore. Are we going to kill when the killer goes by? Am I
still a man? Is he a man, or a beast . . .

—Can I still know anger? Will I raise his visor? Does
he wear a face?

—I hear an iron foot on the cobbles.

—Arrogant as hell. It could only be he.

—What if, even as I rise to kill, I feel forgiveness
coursing through me like a poison? How does one keep
his blood pure, to do the impure job?

—Let's hide out here in the shadows. We'll trip him
up between us.

(Did they freeze like statuary? did they strike like
men? or did eternity show them, at the moment of
truth, another vocation?)

NO HUMANS ON FRIDAY

THERE WAS ONCE a group of people in a certain city who took themselves quite seriously. That is to say:

—the trouble with you is, you could hear in their temples on a given day, the trouble with you is you don't take things seriously enough. Children don't take parents seriously, beatniks don't take generals, the poor don't take poverty, students don't take school, people don't take religion.

—Nothing takes, the intellectuals said fretfully. Everything's getting unstuck.

And that wasn't all. From the point of view of religion, this people had it made, in principle. They were the One Time Religion. Their books said so. The trouble was, there was a certain group around, their minds turned by God knows what rotten wind, who kept complaining . . .

—We don't know about you, but we don't have anything made. Furthermore (and this one really hit low) we don't think you do either.

It all spelled trouble. There was a tank of sacred carp on the imperial grounds. The fish, of course, could never be killed or eaten. On the contrary, they were usually fed on humans; troublesome slaves, persistent thieves, now

79

and then an anarchist or poet. And once a week, on Friday, a succulent maiden.

The fish were crucial to the national well-being. It went like this. When in the course of nature a carp expired (old age or gout were usually diagnosed) he was hauled reverently ashore with a block and tackle, set up in grandeur on a marble catafalque, and his pale belly unseamed. Then the ceremony began. The deacons played out the intestines from the aperture, a shining lifeline of blue, length after bulbous length. They wound the tripe, miles of it, it seemed, round and round a golden spindle. Whenever he would, the chief priest gave a signal and the ceremony stopped; it all depended on his seeing something of import, it was never clear what: an intersection, a grafting, an embolism, a change of bulk or color or odor. Whatever it was, it was God's will, and he spelled it out.

Well, how could all this conceivably raise a storm? There had been no change in the ceremony for centuries. Indeed the very notion of change, of crisis, was repugnant to a people whose blood-letting was controlled by immemorial custom, whose violence when wrought at all, had immediate biblical justification. Jonah, Leviathan shadowed their pool, grey hallowed ghosts of pre-history.

Nonetheless. It must be recorded that one feast day, as the rites proceeded, a most terrifying event occurred. And it occurred in such wise as could not easily be dismissed as the fruit of madness, infiltration, or youth. No, it was our own powers failed us, it was we who shook the heavens and brought ourselves to ruin, or nearly so.

The ceremony was well on, the soundless winding of the sacred intestines proceeded. The worshippers pressed closer and closer to the scene, it was we ourselves who were being landed out of the secular air, out of time and place, by the sacred fish. He lay there, bearded as a pharaoh, wrapt in immortal longings, veiled like a sacrament in his velvet smile. The great jaws were shut like a man-trap on the thin air of death.

The priest had not spoken, the rite was all but over. We hung breathless and nervy. Had the god, for once, nothing to say to us?

No. But would to God, nothing. For since that day, no peace in the city, no peace in the home, and if one can judge by unnatural disordered conduct of good men, no peace in the marital bed.

That day, the priest, as though at great cost, and in spite of himself, red and black in face and all but possessed with anguish, had cried:

—Hail ye, hear ye, the great fish god decrees; from this day, no eating of humans on Friday.

A tide of furious resentment has arisen to balk the oracle. Fifty to sixty per cent of the people, as a recent poll indicates, wish the word invalidated and the priest removed. Extreme elements are calling for his death on a Friday, in atonement. Specialists at the University are hinting broadly at scarcely sublimated urges of a celibate clergy. A poet, a few maidens have spontaneously offered themselves as victims. The carp breeders have published a study; it declares that human flesh is indispensable to fish. It is their chief brain food, it accounts for intestinal fortitude and sound elimination.

So the battle rages. Only a fond man would dare predict its ending. We are left, those of us for whom liturgy was the heart of life, left—with what?

With this. Last Saturday the men who feed the carp came as usual at dawn. They discovered to their astonishment that the waters of the pool were red with blood. In accord with a recent decree there had of course been no Friday immolation. But a maiden's body was floating in the crimson water, crowned with flowers, mad and beautiful as Ophelia. It was surmised that she had offered herself to death during the night hours; but she lay there untouched, she had died of fear or failure of heart. The fish were huddled, sullen, restless and mysteriously sated, at the far end of the pool.

It was only some hours later that we discovered the truth. The head, fins and tail of the largest of our gods were floating just below the surface of the water. Poor, inarticulate, blind, disgorged, lost limbs seeking their habitation. We gathered at the water's edge. No need of priests. Each man, struck to the heart, could read the auspices written in water; lost faith seeking its source.

II PRAYERS

PRAYER OF THE VINDICATED

Thank you at last. The question indeed
was long and vexed, allowing of
infinite delay, this or that stab at solution
well-intentioned, in long run unavailing.

Then the state gathered strength out of weakness,
a dynastic leopard starved itself for the feast.
A people known in the world for its achievement;
coals, gases, alkaloids, engines, boots
and amenities more precise and cunning—
false teeth, false hair, the reprocessing of
old bones and bottles, melting down of jewelry—
a genius to make the head spin in the telling!

Well, we were a chosen people
once more chosen! The gears ground fine
the fires were stoked. Our children
included
in the vast 'definitive solution',
swept along, a minor debris—shoes, scraps of clothing,
a scrawled diary—in the universal tide,
crying like caged birds
at the railroad sidings,
shoved like matzoth trays
into the ovens.

We came too, cajoled
to the same ruin. The smoke stood up
here and there in the faultness sky, a ghetto baking
before sabbath eve.

Chosen! the winch squeals like a tortured
animal, the wine press oozes red.
Chosen! the rings stripped from the womens' fingers,
the mailed bridegroom; Jahweh, our God a consuming
        fire!

PRAYER ON THE SIX P.M. SUBWAY

unsteady
my prayer mounts or falls   why do I
waste so   want so
O make room
in the kingdom of light for lack lusters
among the austere and severe
for malfunctioning men
only this to their credit   NO GREAT HARM DONE
our passage writes
MAYBE on water

nevertheless
might make it yet
who knows   who knows
whether some hour
turns us on
unbelievable
as Christ's new somersaulting
start   his words   his heart

PRAYER FROM THE CATBIRD SEAT

will you   for a space of days
refuse my games
be yourself mercilessly
be serious in the world   uncorrupted by our gods
stand unwavering
beside the faulty and perplexed
the ridden and victimized
speak modestly   act audaciously
sing FREEDOM in the teeth of law
be forebearing be equable
under obscene threats
see good
where rumor smells only evil
widen communion   reduce to zero
the no-man's waste of hatred
yes, strike gently the strings
of inarticulate hearts
O be YOURSELF   supersensible
available
overflow
LIFE! a runnel so pure it cleanses
the stables of our foul wills
so deep we are borne along   drowned   ecstatic
metamorphosed out of our sweet skins

are YOU
east or west   poor or in possession

squatter in Watts rotting in jails somnolent suburban
yes
allowing
vicious depredations   against
bone and flesh of BROTHERS?
be ANSWER be QUESTION ABSENCE and PRESENCE
WHEN and WHERE and WHO
O
TERMAGANT of history TIGER overarching
with your electric body our skies
unfended CHILDHOOD intellectual GRANDEUR
SCOPE beyond compassing!
come EASTER
FLOWERS BIRDS FLYING TREES and MEN
erase with your mouth to mouth respiration
the mortician smile of death
come PEACE and SWORD
break the locked fists of dominations
upon our throats
come SURGEON knit into one
cunning anthropos the bones bones dry bones
slack jaws scattered knees
of the amnesiac dead
come desert SUN
suck into nothing
our brackish
serpentine joys
come STIGMATIC
write on our blue eyeballs
words you learned by heart
in death's hideous limbo
where none but you escaped
his overkill arrogant reach
GLORY GLORY GLORY

PRAYER FROM A BACK PEW

O GOD YOU HAVE DECLARED TO ALL THE
CHILDREN OF YOUR CHURCH BY THE
VOICE OF YOUR HOLY PROPHETS

> *Well I don't know, at least I wonder. One kid dead,*
> *the old man out of work, the girl on the town not*
> *coming home at all. You get to wonder. If the check*
> *doesn't come I*

THAT THROUGH THE WHOLE EXTENT OF
YOUR DOMINION YOU ARE THE SOWER OF
GOOD SEED AND THE GROWER OF

> *stand in line all afternoon; ache, varicose, dread.*
> *"Good seed and chosen vines!" I haven't seen*
> *anything green in years, the drought kills*

CHOSEN VINES. GRANT TO YOUR PEOPLE
WHOM YOU HAVE SYMBOLICALLY CALLED
YOUR VINE AND HARVEST

> *it all off. You don't ask for much but*
> *it does seem hard—"thorns and briars."*
> *I know. You have less and less to*

THAT WITH ALL THORNS AND BRIARS
  REMOVED THEY MAY BE WORTHY TO
  BRING FORTH GOOD FRUIT IN
  ABUNDANCE

> *give—you just make it. Less joy, that's the*
> *worst of all. "Good fruit in*

THROUGH OUR LORD JESUS CHRIST YOUR
  SON WHO LIVES AND REIGNS GOD
  FOREVER AND EVER.   AMEN.

> *abundance"—a pound of spotted apples, a*
> *soup bone, some marrow. I can tell you next*
> *year's meals, years and years.*
> *But we'll get there I know.*
> *Through Christ*
> *our Lord. That's the word that sticks. Sometimes*
> *in your craw, sometimes in your heart. The boys bought*
> *me an Easter plant. It'll be on the table, white and*
> *green and all. You don't need much.*

PRAYER OF THE THIRD MAN

I PASSED THE wounded phoenix in the ditch, passed him twice, two aeons, two sins. A third time (it says) I come again; outcaste, beat, wrong skin, wrong god. To do at length what must be done—the wrong thing?

Too easy, too right at first. So I could do nothing. A sea change must cut me loose, even from him. He was too near. When I came up, he twitched and knew. Jew to Jew, white to white. Blood told; too alike, too easy. The current broke, we fell apart.

O more time was needed; he must be nearer death, among the bluebottles and worms convening upon his flesh. And I must be nearer—what?

I did not know. I only knew—the first and second times were wrong. Blood told, told wrong. My blood sank back like a tiger's, waiting a better prey. My mercy slept among mercies. There was bigger game ahead, or none at all. But not this.

Go away then, and come back; not three of us; one. A priest, his shadow; then at length, a man. How long, how long that takes!

How long that takes! His wounds worsening, death crawling over him. Night and day, no help. The road empty, every tree awake, every leaf listening—a footfall? someone's return?

I came back. Outcaste, outsmarted. Claims, big talk, brass, all forgotten. What a light baggage the gospel was, floating on my guts like no food at all, the book vanished like bread on the tides! Nothing left; some small instinct, turning my eyes his way, fastening me to him; O there was no letting go!

I knelt beside him, the ditch side of a mountain road. Mercy was a judgment, delayed until I could win. I drank it like a sheaf of flowers. It flowed over, a suppuration, the untended flesh of Christ, married to mine. Heavy, heavy, a sheaf drenched in rot and dew, corn too heavy for the gleaner; shucks, leaves, grain, all spoiled.

To be judged this way; to price my survival! The world upside down, angry angels cranking the wheel. Who saves who? a half mad muttering in my ear, a cry, a violated man, the whirling anguish of the universe! I knelt there, fastened to him, a rain of rotting gold. The storm broke over me, bore me down, the dumb sticks dancing like a witch's choir.

This was it. We went straight up, all the scenery; ass, cross, corn, flesh, me. The napkin of the universe closed its four corners, a grab bag for heaven to sort out. The question groaning, clanking, braying, a levitated ass; WHO ARE YOU BALAAM?

SUBURBAN PRAYER

Grant us for grace
oppositions, stimyings
sand in our pet gears
a bubble in the cozy blood

Crowd our real estate
with the rag tag real, the world.
Marry us off, lonely girls
to Harlem and Asia. This Lent
celebrate in the haunted house, the world.

PRAYER FOR THE MORNING HEADLINES

MERCIFULLY GRANT PEACE IN OUR DAYS. THROUGH YOUR HELP MAY WE BE FREED FROM PRESENT DISTRESS . . . HAVE MERCY ON WOMEN AND CHILDREN HOMELESS IN FOUL WEATHER, RANTING LIKE BEES AMONG GUTTED BARNS AND STILES. HAVE MERCY ON THOSE (LIKE US) CLINGING ONE TO ANOTHER UNDER FIRE, TERROR ON TERROR, GRAPES THE GRAPE SHOT STRIKES. HAVE MERCY ON THE DEAD, BEFOULED, TRODDEN LIKE SNOW IN HEDGES AND THICKETS. HAVE MERCY, DEAD MAN, WHOSE GRANDIOSE GENTLE HOPE DIED ON THE WING, WHOSE BODY STOOD LIKE A TREE BETWEEN STRIKE AND FALL, STOOD LIKE A CRIPPLE ON HIS WOODEN CRUTCH. WE CRY: HALT! WE CRY: PASSWORD! DISHONORED HEART, REMEMBER AND REMIND, THE OPEN SESAME: FROM THERE TO HERE, FROM INNOCENCE TO US: HIROSHIMA DRESDEN GUERNICA SELMA SHARPEVILLE COVENTRY DACHAU. INTO OUR HISTORY, PASS! SEED HOPE. FLOWER PEACE.

PRAYER FROM A WHITE SKIN

Where we have lighted
the rehearsing fires of hell
let a tear
from the furious eye of the poor
fall, extinguishing.
Unwind   unwind
the cerements that bind
Lazarus
hand and foot in his flesh
his guilt large
on absurd phylacteries;
skin   win   white   right.
A black face rives the stone
"COME FORTH TO THE LORD'S DAY."

PRAYER FROM A PICKET LINE

Bring the big guardian
angels or devils in black
jackets and white casques
into the act at last. *Love, love at the end.*

The landholders withholding
no more; the jails springing
black and white Easter men;
truncheons like lilies, hoses
gentle as baby pee. *Love, love at the end.*

Bishops down in the ranks
mayors making it too.
Sheriff meek as a shorn lamb
smelling like daisies, drinking dew.
Love, love at the end.

PRAYER FOR THE BIG MORNING

People my heart
with the living! their cries like
fists, their sight healing
my eyes foreclosing night.
Would be
that one and populous
heart of man;
O cries like fists
O sight set free!

III MEDITATIONS

Bob Fitch—a *lāos* photo

MEDITATION ON A PHOTOGRAPH

THE OLD MAN is brought to birth on the shoulders of the young. Alleluia! That was a great hour—one man, one vote. Or (to say the same thing) no death, never again death!

Even if I die tomorrow, how can I ever die? This body, tanned like a Jew's in Egypt, is risen up, is borne onward. O my people!

A long exile, the wheel of a chariot on your neck, slavery in the fields, slavery in the streets, mockery, defeat, silence. Manhood without honor, fear, behind the closed shutters. A man grows older, death springs from his side. A man grows older, without ever having been a man. A man grows older—what else is he to do? Like the shoe on his foot, like the horse on his reins; old shoe, old horse, old man, where are you bound for? Old leather, old hooves, Old Black Joe, why were you ever born? Who ever wanted you? Who ever gave a damn?

The cottonfields did, the magnolias did, the sweet sun-burned sloe-eyed Nigras did. Come to think of it, we did, too. Stephen Foster said we did. Let's see now; "Southern culture, admirable for its stability, its horizons, its sense of the land, its humanism, its—" well, it requires something very simple, son; a nigger, a horse, a pair of Sunday shoes. A weekday nigger in the fields, a Sunday nigger for the Lord. Jesus, you tell 'em. Let us pray this boy never gets uppity, your divine scheme of salvation never gets distempered by carpetbaggin' communist infiltratin' beatnik disorganizers comin' down here (welcome to the magnolia state, welcome to the bayous, welcome to Southern womanhood) insinuatin' their disastrous immoral hunkerin' ways. . .

We died, lots of us died. It was always death, death was a hired hand sweating in the fields at your left hand, black as you. When you straightened up, he squatted down, quick as a coon at feeding time. And when you bent down—you never knew but he straightened up like a blade, he had you! One swipe of the hook, one twist of the cord; there you were among the sacks, stuffed in like corn or cotton, bound for the river bed. Sleep sound, nigger.

Where's Joe, where's Tom, where's Ez? Shut up boy, shut up wench. Get in the house, douse the light. Now it was like this, this is what we saw. . .

Oh lots and lots of us died. That was bad and good too. I mean as time went on there were less of us to live and given everything, that was good. And there were less men left to die; that was a mercy too.

Some of us made 60, it was easy. But look around at 80. It's like a tree, standing in mid-forest after a fire. Alone, or almost. My God, what winds those were, hot as hell's chimney. Now I'm black for sure, now I'm hurt. Will next spring see me standing? And if so, what for? Dumb as a tree. Why stand up at all? Because someone planted me here years ago and no one cut me down yet. No one needs my death. Forgotten by the hired hand, a hell of a reason to live.

Now I'm 103. How old is a rock, the only rock in the middle of a plowed field? Too much trouble moving it— let the niggers plow and plant and harvest around it. Leave it alone. Act as though it wasn't there. Weird isn't it, come to think of it, one rock standing in a 20-acre field? They say years ago a farmer put a 10-mule team on it to pull it down—broke the ropes every time. Funny, it don't look that strong.

I am that strong. Time goes by, a man turns to water or he turns to stone. Water, they tip you over, they pour you out. Boy come here, boy go there, boy kneel down. Nigger was you at that meeting? Take off your shirt. Pull his pants off him. We'll show this uppity—You'll talk? Leave him go. Now boy make it fast. Who was there, what did they say? You spill it boy or we'll spill you— guts and all.

Some spilled it. They were water. Watered-down men. I tell you, when you saw that branding iron, that big stick, that circle of eyes and hoods you made your mind up quick. You peed your pants and spilled what you knew—or you turned to stone.

It wasn't like choosing this or that, black or white, life or death. It was more like choosing between one death and another. How do you want to die? Cracked in two like a rock or spilled out like water? C'mon nigger make up your fool mind. We ain't got all night.

Well it's a dry time. You don't see anyone my age around, no more than last year's rain. But here I am. Not much, but here. See how easy the boys raise me up? Not

much left, a skinny rat of a man, an old branch, a knot
of leaves.

You should have seen what I was once. They couldn't
budge me, more than 10 mules could. Ever see men split
a rock, build a fire under it, pour cold water on it? Ever
been burned, scalded? I cracked all right. The biggest
part of me died there, more than half of me. But I kept
my mouth shut and walked away. I was still a man. I'd
chosen—my kind of death over theirs. I spat blood and
grinned to myself and thought alleluia tomcat, eight lives
to go.

One hundred and three. The hundred is serious, the
three is a joke. I'm not much bigger than a three-year-old
Jesus. I've stooped so often into doorways out of the
burning noon and the clay hot as bricks under foot, into
that hush and cool, where the mother's cries grow still
and the newborn cry is raised. I've thought every time,
why child we made it again. And the mouth like a little
dog's open with a yap of surprise tasting the sweet air like
milk, crying what's the world like old man, old man?
C'mon honey, I'll show you around.

One hundred and three. The hundred is serious. I've
got scars to show it. No fun turning into a tree that's
turning into stone. And still be a man!

The three's a joke. The jokers came around today.
C'mon grandpa, you're old enough to vote now. We'll
take you downtown and get registered.

I don't move easy. I was sitting in the sun holding that
child. He felt good as gold, he slept there like a flower,
why should I put him down for all the world. They said
grandpa it's serious. It's for us all. I said to myself, it's
always been for you, everything's for you. My bones tell
me I'm on a different errand, go register yourselves. They

nagged away, Grandpa it's for him too. You want him to have the life you had? Dirt cabin, slaving for nothing, jail for nothing, running like a dog when they snap the whip, no say, no nothing?

They had me there. I put the child down then like you put aside something precious when danger comes near. His mother took him.

So here I am hoisted around town like a halloween pope, tasting honey and milk in my mouth like old Moses, tears in my eyes. I'm registered now. Merry Christmas Mister Sheriff, Mister Jail, Mister Firehose, Mister Dog, Mister Death. God rest you merry. O what my eyes have seen!

THE BARGAIN

THE SCENE IS the visiting room of a federal jail.

I have a friend, to whom my relationship is complex as the internal system of a human being. I am to him as bellows to heart, as hand to mouth, as cowardice to action, as purveyor to stolen fruit, as cleric to civilian and saint. I know mine and mine know me.

We play a game sometimes. It always starts in the same way. I appear at the prison with a notebook in hand. I ask him—occupation?

The figure on the bench stirs. His eyes are used to mine, but he is ill at ease today. My clothing fits my frame, but his is like a flophouse gift. More than that, there is a wall between us, invisible and brutal. The horse we all ride has tossed him on the far side of the law, his life has begun paying for it, but he has not yet picked up the pieces. I am still on my mount, looking down at him, the maladroit casualty.

But he answers me—Onetime short-order cook, dishwasher, delivery boy, doorman, jakes attendant.

First offense?

Yes.

Name the charge. I want him to say it. There is nothing for love or hatred quite so healthy as forcing a man to articulate his crime. True or not, it makes things clear. A certain acceptance of reality. A subtle way of underscoring the difference between number one and number two. It draws the poison out of heroism and friendship—all those human foibles with which we pretend to transcendence.

Non-cooperation in war. Contempt of court. Burning of draft card. He said it flatly and gently, his voice suggested a run-down of symptoms in a public clinic by a man who no longer cared that they were his symptoms. A man lives too long with waiting, with humiliation. Disinterest in patient, disinterest presumed in doctor, I wrote.

What brought you to this?

He lifted his shoulders. My whole life.

I had taken down only a line or two. I was in the presence of someone who interested me—a dead man, gray as Lazarus, sitting in a gray mausoleum of a room, his clothing tossed on him from four winds indifferently. Yet he was stubbornly functioning in a queer vertical way, a way that suggested something living.

Was it not time for reasonableness?—Look, I said half to myself, half to him. We are two civilized men who have opted differently during a time of crisis. You for jail, I for whatever normalcy, whatever freedom I can salvage. I believe with the kind of passion your act brands as impure, that I can bring the sodden hulk to shore, can save some lives, can save some order and legitimacy. But for me to do something with my choice and for you to do something with yours, we need to undergo a change of assignment, some adjustment of the rules. Will you try it?

Go ahead. He sat there, like nothing in this world, like a dead man. As though what we name life had already

done a mortician's job on him, opened his veins, propped
him up, a cheap welfare corpse.

What I'm really after—will you take the part of a
condemned man? I was growing unseemly and eager. All
my social science was running for cover. I leaned forward
—I need, I need, in order to do what I have to do, someone whose death is imminent and unjust, at least in his
own mind. I need an innocence no court can disabuse or
corrupt. I need a sentence of death. I need you—to be
pushed that far. Will you do it—and then will you talk?

He would. He said he would. Sitting there, it was hard
to believe he seriously saw any need of a change of masks.
What had killed him, had killed him. What kept him before me, incandescent and vigilant, drew on its own
sources, worked from its own laws.

Listen then, I began. Consider for a moment this
fiction. I am, let us say, for the sake of somewhere to begin, an indifferent cleric in a large city. I am ill. The
name of my sickness is history. I live on the debris of
twenty buried cities, twenty centuries. Everything durable
in them is ground to powder, everything soft is become
inflammable. Am I a cynic for imaging the fact? The
sacred word for my neighborhood is tradition. But the
truth is, I have pitched my tent on the filth and debris
of time. The locus for my tragicomedy is the city dump.
An underground fire runs through it; it seldom reaches
the surface in flame. Its presence is marked like a vein of
coal or oil, by the choking disease-bearing atmosphere. I
am dying in my place. I am assured by the authorities,
even by the ancestral spirits, that it is a good thing to die
in such a way, in this place. When I poke the god in his
rib for an oracle, his answer is already alive in me, awakened, I suspect, by the temple menu of roots and herbs.

He says, stay where you are. But I suspect he wants me
here because he himself is immobilized. I bring him his
beer and rattle the prayer wheel. We must look busy; it
is in the rule book.

Our day is as exciting as Mrs. Wiggs' in her cabbage
patch. Monday we sweep the temple, Tuesdays we check
the plumbing, Wednesdays we empty the votive bowls
and count the offerings, Thursdays we mount the roof
and scrape the pigeon dirt from the gargoyles, Fridays we
go down to the poor bearing baskets whose cost is reck-
oned at 10 per cent of the take, Saturday is Overseas
Consciousness day. Sundays—but need I go on?

Christ! I burst out, I am stuffed like a capon with
sacred routine. I never chose to eat it, I never digested it,
they shoved it up my other end. But you now, you've
taken my bargain. You have presumably only a few hours
to live, you dare a great deal. I'm not interested, I think
you must sense, in the eunuch in the Pantheon. But I
suppose you love life, I suppose you secrete it and tip it
over, and create it anew. I suppose . . .

Correct, said the other. I get your idea. You give me
twenty-four hours. There is, of course, some adjustment
to make. (He was the despair of me, the apologetic
mouth, the unskilled hands, the fifth from the end in line
for a meal, his frame built up like a shack from left-
overs, from soup bones, the hand-out life, the misfit
clothing.)

Twenty-four hours. I think . . . (He had a kind of hang-
man's humor, he pressed in on me mockingly, from the
other side of the coffin.) I think I would blow it all on a
meal with a few friends. No crepe hanging, no lining up
for goodbyes. But plenty of wine, some good food. Something of myself. Something to remember, for them and

me. I think I could go off to whatever it was after that. I
don't want to sound inflated; but I suspect a man's guts
don't crawl so with the horror of death, if they have
some red wine in them.

How about a message, though? Would you leave them
a message?

He laughed, the first time; I didn't like it. He was
sauce for the goose and the gander too. He sat there, 150
pounds, 5 feet 11, and he laughed in a most transported
way. When he did that you asked, had the man ever
done anything else?

I wanted to be a skeptic though. He hadn't proved anything yet, he was wrapped in the hazards of his choice, no
winner, not even the glamour of a loser.

You wouldn't laugh, I chided, if the thing were real.
Or if you really dug into the New Testament. But you're
phony; you're making your own kind of peace—don't you
know death brings on words like a cataract at the end of a
millpond? A man can't rush them out fast enough. John
says so, one-fourth of his gospel.

John says so. (He mocked my form-*geschichte*.) But
who says He said what John said? I think they had a din-
ner together all right, and then some! But I mean something else. Look, friend. He had turned the wick high
again, his eyes were all alight in his clay. It's what they
heard His whole life say that counts. That's what we have
of Him. Something transparent, something running,
springs in the desert. You have to stop to hear. Such a
man speaks through his pores, he writes on the air, there
is nothing, nothing about him but eloquence.

And then the idiocy and fever of belief. They literally
heard things; a life going by like a circus cart, a calliope

grinding out music, a car crowded with clowns. One life, imagine, crying out, beckoning, *Come on! Get with it!* Running through burning hoops, stopping short, making U-turns in the lions' cage, choosing the unlikeliest moment to speak the most absurd things. And all of it fitting, intersecting, making sense, dissolving again, accepted, violated, cast aside, befouled, confronted, put to death.

John said He said *peace* that night. Maybe He did. But isn't the point a different one? A man's mouth can say peace while his hands are saying something else, reaching for something else. You have to break him to find out what he's made of. I mean dynamite or bread. I don't know how else. All the rest is—a reversal, a wrong order of things. You take a man at his word; but who deserves that, when maybe the unborn are going to burn for it? Let's see how a man dies, then we'll have an inkling, then let the news, good news or bad, out.

Holy Week. Sweet friend (he could smile like a tiger, he could kill. But he put his hand out to me with a strange gentle fervor.) The exterminators gather on a Pacific island, savage and civilized; different speech, one method, different timing, one game. They shake the palm branch before the world, its pollen drifts on the Trade Winds, peace, peace, a germ war. Holy Week is on us. The bombers go out, their asperges of fire. Do you wonder? (His glance took in the room, as though he had done it himself, the bars, the poverty, the cold.) I have left the jungle, I prefer the cage. It is not to keep them out, it is to keep—faith.

Would it have been better if He had never lived or died in a way that makes it true? He said *shalom, not as the world gives do I give.* What does it mean to lead others into consciousness, that pure incendiary oxygen, where all choices, all intoxications, all follies are in the air?

But I cried out—I am sick unto death of the load of history in my bowels. And you offer me, instead, a fundamentalist life, all major virtues except love.

That may be. He was exasperating, untouchable. It all ricocheted off him.

He was like the shield of a pagan warrior—a skin no arrow could pierce.

Let me go on, he said. You decreed it, my time is short. But I cannot help thinking, He ordered peace, His friends understood it. He had given a certain push, a direction to life; something new in the air, men who healed, an end of the universal poison. How long did it last? How long before the earth swallowed him whole? Were the new power systems more humane because they were stamped with a cross?

You have to dig very deep to know, you fear as you dig, sick unto death of the skeleton that may await the next thud of the pick. Has time buried everything that pretends to judge and tame? I mean peace. He looked around, with a gesture. The room was like a monstrous external organ, something gone wrong, something nature would have made of tissue, miniscule within his body, an iron lung. As it was, his prison, his salvation.

Would not some men be like me, to this day, even if He had not started it all? I do not mean to be hopeless, I only want the language to have a more modest base.

You want God left out of it?

He has already opted out of it. So the rhetoric is in the

strictest sense diabolic. Peace, peace. There are fanatics and cross bearers who will kill for peace until the last man is ground under.

But the time really is short. How I wish it were possible to make of our bargain the truth of things!—a good deal less bumbling, less expensive, less embarrassing for church and state—a definitive solution in fact. But one does his best. In this case, if we cannot walk into the silence of death, at least let us keep quiet and allow our lives to speak for us.

The buzzer sounded, the guard was at the door. My friend pressed my hand.—Shalom. As a Friend once said; see you next Sunday.

BREAD

Want nothing small about men—except perhaps their words, modest and thoughtful and almost inaudible before their deeds. For the rest, bigness; heart, brain. Imagination too; let it take the world in two hands and show us what it's like to BE! Tell us about it, we're hungry. Doesn't the Bible call truth BREAD? We're starved, our smile has lost out, we crawl on a thin margin—a life, maybe, but so what? Where's the man who says *yes*, says *no*, like a thunderclap? Where's the man whose *no* turns to *yes* in his mouth—he can't deny life, he asks like a new flower or a new day or a hero even: What more is there to love than I have loved?

When I hear bread breaking, I see something else; it seems almost as though God never meant us to do anything else. So beautiful a sound, the crust breaks up like manna and falls all over everything, and then we EAT; bread gets inside humans. It turns into what the experts call "formal glory of God." But don't let that worry you. Sometime in your life, hope you might see one starved man, the look on his face when the bread finally arrives. Hope you might have baked it or bought it—or even needed it yourself. For that look on his face, for your hands meeting his across a piece of bread, you might be

114

willing to lose a lot, or suffer a lot—or die a little, even. "Formal glory"; well yes. Maybe what we're trying to understand is what they're trying to say, who knows? I don't think they understand—or every theologian would be working part time in a bread line. Who knows who might greet him there or how his words might change afterward—like stones into bread? Most theologians have never broken bread for anyone in their lives. Do you know, I think they think Christ is as well fed as His statues.

But I don't know. Man keeps breaking in.

Take your "typical man" across the world. Let him in. Look at him, he isn't white, he probably isn't clean. He certainly isn't well fed or American, or Christian. So then what? What's left? Well, maybe now we're getting somewhere; Christ is all that's left, if you're looking for a mystery. He's real as a man. Don't just stand there! Sit him down. Offer him some bread! He'll understand that; bread comes across. So does Christ—Luke says so—in the breaking of bread. What a beautiful sound—try and see!

I keep thinking of that poor man. And his face, when someone shows up against all odds to treat him like a human being. But that isn't all, or even half the truth. The other half, or more, is what he sees in *you*. And that's a mercy, because Christ is merciless about the poor. He wants them around—always, and everywhere. He's condemned them to live with us. It's terrifying. I mean for us, too. It's not only that we are ordered, rigorously ordered, to serve the poor. That's hard enough; Christ gives so few orders in all the gospel. But the point is, what the poor see in us—and don't see, too. We stand there, American, White, Christian, with the keys of the kingdom and the keys of the world in our pocket. Everything

about us says: *Be like me! I've got it made.* But the poor
man sees the emperor—naked. Like the look of Christ,
the poor man strips us down to the bone.

And then, if we're lucky, something dawns—even on
us. Why, we're the poor. The reel plays backward, everything's reversed when the gospel is in the air. The clothes
fly off Dives; he's Negro, he's nothing, he's got his hand
out—forever. Empty as a turned-up skull. Watch the
reel now—it's important to see which way the bread is
passing. To you, to me! We're in luck. This is our day.

The poor have it hard, the saying goes. Well, we're
the hardest thing they have. Do you know I think sometime if we poor rich are ever going to grow up into faith,
it will be only because poor men are around—everywhere,
always, drunks, winos, junkeys, the defeated, the ne'er-do-
wells, those who didn't make it onto our guarded spoiled
playground. And those who never wanted to play our
game, and whose rags are therefore a kind of riches we
will never wear. All of them, a special Providence, a holy
rain and sun, falling equally on the unjust, the smooth
conmen, the well oiled Cadillac humans and inhumans,
the purblind, the Christians and their impure gods in cup-
boards and banks and nuclear silos, the white unchristian
West, all of us. But for the poor, we'd never know who
we are, or where we came from or where we are (just
possibly) going—in spite of tons of catechisms and the
ten editions of the *Handbook for Instant Salvation* and
that best of sellers, *I Kept You-Know-Who Out and
Found God.*

On the Cloud of Unknowing; number nine. Blind as
bats. Then a poor man (they are all miracle men, they
have to be to live one day in our world) stands there. His
poverty is like a few loaves and fishes—enough for every-

one! He breaks and breaks bread and feeds us and we line up again and again, literally bottomless with our need, going for broke, sore and ill tempered and jostling one another, hearing the word pass down the line, *there's hardly any left*, resenting, straining forward in a frenzy of despair. But there's always enough, always some more. Christ guaranteed it—I don't know why. The poor you have always with you. Like a marvelous majestic legacy of God. His best possession, in our hands. Undeserved, like the Eucharist. *O send someone in from the gate where Dives sits on a dungheap in his sores, send even one of the dogs to whimper for us—Would Lazarus of his heart's goodness let a dog lick up the crumbs from the floor, and carry even in a dog's mouth something for the damned?*

This is the truth about the world, our Lord said. Everything comes right, all the deep wrongs of existence are turned inside out, the rich are stripped even of their shrouds, the poor men go in wedding garments.

The first way to defeat Christianity is to strike Christians blind. Let the rich really think they can hang on to it all, and wheeler deal even with the angel of judgment named Christ, and (imagine) face Him for the first time in death—when all of life is a great tragic Greek chorale sung by Christs in masks, sometimes furies, sometimes war-racked women. Sometimes a foul wino in a mission sings it out like a bird of paradise remembering his last incarnation, but never, never looks up when Mr. Big goes by. The untranslated, unbearable cry, pure judgment, pure anger, pure rejection. *Reality! Reality!*

O the poor will line up before the Judge with Torrid Eyes, a handful of daisies in one hand, a sword in the other. They look gently toward His right side. They know. *Come.* They were the workers of corporal mercy. They are saved for having been, for being, for being for others. They save even us. They carried fresh bread to stale lives. *Come, beloved of My Father.*